D1532369

WITHDRAWN
FROM THE RECORDS OF THE
MID-CONTINENT PUBLIC LIBRARY

650.1 SU24
Sue, Marsha Petrie.
The reactor factor

MID-CONTINENT PUBLIC LIBRARY
Kearney Branch
100 S. Platte-Clay Way
Kearney, MO 64060

KE

Praise for *The Reactor Factor*

"With all the wake-up calls we seem to have forced on us today, it is delightful to read an author that shoots straight about how to be ready for the next wake-up call. If you're a little nervous about your relevance in today's economy, you really should read this book."
—Gary Sitton, President and Founder, SunGard Technologies (retired)

"Marsha has a knack for effectively holding up the mirror that reflects not only our reality, but also our potential . . . while gently reminding us, the choice is ours."
—Gwen Gallagher, President, Old Republic Home Protection

"*The Reactor Factor* identifies behaviors by employees, managers, executives, and even companies that are detrimental to successful outcomes of their endeavors and also offers ways of remedying those behaviors. Self-reliance rather than self-indulgence is key to positive change. This book should be required reading for all politicians."
—Don Slotten, Entrepreneur and Marsha's High School
    Homeroom Teacher

"Once again Marsha gets to the heart of good business practices, leadership, and management. This insightful collection of wisdom from successful business veterans is just as valid in boom times as they are in turbulent and uncertain times. Job well done, Marsha!"
—Michael D. Austin, President, Armor Sports Holdings

"Marsha is real. Her commonsense approach and reality check on everyday life is a breath of fresh air. I could read or listen to her every day to get that shot in the arm straight talk that keeps me on track."
—Wendy Rice-Isaacs, Regional Administrative Director, Vorys, Sater,
    Seymour, and Pease, LLP

"Marsha provides *the* blueprint for peak performance at work. If you want to make more money more easily and want to learn to smile knowingly at conflict and office politics in the knowledge that you are fully equipped to deal with everything that comes your way, you simply must buy this book. It would be ludicrous not to."
—Mike Giles, CEO, Standing on the Shoulders of Giants,
   United Kingdom

"Marsha's new book provides direct talk to those who want to achieve their purpose and potential in all sides of life. It is rich in the range of subjects that can bring out the best in us in dealing with others, situations and successful outcomes. This book will be one you rely on for a very long time to come."
—James W. Myers, CEO, Myers Management & Capital Group, Inc.

"OK. Where do I start? Wow? How about Bam? Slam? Smash? If you are looking for niceties, sweetness, and courtesies—*The Reactor Factor* is not the place to visit. If your skin is thick and you think 'YOU can handle the TRUTH!'—then you have come to the right place. I pride myself on not being too politically correct. Marsha is making me feel like a little old lady for not having come out with this book myself. *The Reactor Factor* makes sense. Quit your sniffing, get to reading, and plan on making some changes."
—Rick Gillis, Host of Rick Gillis Employment Radio, and Author of
   Really Useful Job Search Tactics

"Marsha Petrie Sue shows us if we simply react to difficult forces and events around us, we adopt a victim mentality. However, she calls it as she sees it, and invites us to take these so-called 'troubled times' as 'times of opportunity.' You grab the opportunity, you wrestle it, and you take charge. Isn't that preferable to falling in a helpless heap? Take hope, take heed, take hold!"
—Dr. Geoff Haw, Managing Director, Sagacity Services, Australia

"A must-read for aspiring and self-confident leaders and managers that are focused on sustainable career growth by recognizing, avoiding, and benefiting from individual and organizational behaviors that can stymie all but the strongest and adaptable talents."
—Arch Granda, President, Grandwest and Associates

"The Reactor Factor lays out a plan that anyone can follow and achieve. Her no-nonsense approach to developing a straightforward and effective workplace game plan is essential to taking control of your career and your life!"
—Kelly Zitlow, CMPS®, Vice President, Suburban Mortgage, Inc.

"For anyone in management *this book is a must*. Marsha Petrie Sue continues to inform in a clever, humorous way that directly gets to the useful information necessary to reduce stress and increase production. Our patients are pleased that our staff is happy and efficient, and I attribute that to applying Ms. Petrie Sue's methods. This latest book compels the healthy outlook on life that we all deserve."
—Bud Rasner, DDS, Owner, Knolls Dental Group

"Only you can start the engine and place the gear into 'Drive' to be able to move forward with the necessary changes required in your life. Marsha's book provides the thought processes on how to make those changes happen. SO WHAT'S STOPPING YOU? MAKE IT HAPPEN! You'll be glad you did!"
—Kathey Dufek, Assistant Vice President, The Doctors Company

"What a great book! Every company leader, manager, and supervisor should read it. Marsha Petrie Sue has created an easy-to-follow road map for getting people to accept personal responsibility for their decisions and actions. How refreshing—no more entitlement mentality!"
—Dr. Tony Alessandra, Keynote Speaker and Author of *The NEW Art of Managing People and Communicating at Work*

"Business people, young and old, can enjoy the successes of maturity and experience through reading, absorbing, and applying the information in this book and your earlier writings. This book provides easily repeatable actions for success. Marsha's provided the playbook; the ball is in your court!!"
—Rick Labrum, Vice President, Wealth Management, SmithBarney

"It's refreshing to see someone so passionate about personal accountability when all you see and hear out there these days is entitlement. Holding yourself accountable is the first step to success. Marsha gives you the tools you need to get it done."
—Bo Calbert, President, McCarthy Building Companies Inc. Southwest

"*The Reactor Factor* contains the wisdom and advice relevant today, and we have seen it in action. Marsha's past consulting services to our company taught us not to react emotionally to economic downturns and to not lose positive focus on business development. Instead, we responded constructively by redeployment of employee skills to increase e-networking to improve our relationship with customers and to personalize our brand."
—John and Anne Draper, Owners, Bear Mountain Ranch

"Well you've done it again, Marsha Petrie Sue. *The Reactor Factor* provides the tools, techniques, and information needed for positive action in any economy. Warning: this book is only for those who choose to move forward in their jobs, business, and life!"
—Janita Cooper, CEO, Master Duplicating Corporation

"Quintessential Marsha Petrie Sue. A book for people who are really serious about taking charge of their careers."
—Ruth. G. Covey, Director of Quality, Security, and Export Control, Armor Designs

"When I hear of a new project tackled by Marsha, I get excited and I can't wait for the results. And she did it again! *The Reactor Factor* is another one of her masterpieces of straightforward talk, a no-nonsense and down-to-earth approach on what needs to be done and what can indeed be achieved. Don't wait for anybody's bailout, read this book, and take charge! The rewards will be immense."
—Danielle Hampson, Talk Show Host, *Mind Your BIZness*

"A great how-to manual on taking control of your life. A real guide to eliminate the excuses blocking you from creating the life of your dreams."
—Randi Smith-Todorowski, President, Atlas Martial Arts

"A survival guide for all times—this should be in everyone's purse, briefcase, home, office, and car. How we make decisions and take action defines the course to success or destruction—you choose, and it happens in an instant! Since the only thing that is certain is change, you'd better get equipped to shape and sharpen your reaction to create your success!"
—Norma Strange, Partner, Residual Income Technologies

"Marsha gets to the point early, as you do when facing crisis and downturn. Attitude, assertion, honest communication, and practical strategies abound in this book. The world needs to hear these more. Very useful for job applicants, job keepers, and employers who want to progress. There is something for everyone in this book. You have no excuse not to read it. This is not only a winner in adversity but it makes sense in good times."
—Penny Barrington Haw, Facilitator, Qualified Coach, Trainer,
   Teacher, Spruiker, Australia

"Marsha's book is an exceptional tool for understanding how you can become and remain successful in today's ever-changing business world. She shows you how to apply yourself in real-world business situations through knowledge sharing, networking, and self-assessment. It is a great supplement to one's bag of business tools."
—Allan T. Zinky, PMP, Service Development Director, American Express Technologies

THE REACTOR FACTOR

THE REACTOR FACTOR

HOW TO HANDLE DIFFICULT WORK SITUATIONS WITHOUT GOING NUCLEAR

MARSHA PETRIE SUE

WILEY

John Wiley & Sons, Inc.

Copyright © 2010 by Marsha Petrie Sue. All rights reserved.

Published by John Wiley & Sons, Inc., Hoboken, New Jersey.
Published simultaneously in Canada.

No part of this publication may be reproduced, stored in a retrieval system, or transmitted
in any form or by any means, electronic, mechanical, photocopying, recording, scanning,
or otherwise, except as permitted under Section 107 or 108 of the 1976 United States
Copyright Act, without either the prior written permission of the Publisher, or
authorization through payment of the appropriate per-copy fee to the Copyright Clearance
Center, Inc., 222 Rosewood Drive, Danvers, MA 01923, (978) 750-8400, fax
(978) 646-8600, or on the web at www.copyright.com. Requests to the Publisher for
permission should be addressed to the Permissions Department, John Wiley & Sons, Inc.,
111 River Street, Hoboken, NJ 07030, (201) 748-6011, fax (201) 748-6008, or online at
http://www.wiley.com/go/permissions.

Limit of Liability/Disclaimer of Warranty: While the publisher and author have used their
best efforts in preparing this book, they make no representations or warranties with respect
to the accuracy or completeness of the contents of this book and specifically disclaim any
implied warranties of merchantability or fitness for a particular purpose. No warranty may
be created or extended by sales representatives or written sales materials. The advice and
strategies contained herein may not be suitable for your situation. You should consult with
a professional where appropriate. Neither the publisher nor author shall be liable for any
loss of profit or any other commercial damages, including but not limited to special,
incidental, consequential, or other damages.

For general information on our other products and services or for technical support, please
contact our Customer Care Department within the United States at (800) 762-2974,
outside the United States at (317) 572-3993 or fax (317) 572-4002.

Wiley also publishes its books in a variety of electronic formats. Some content that appears
in print may not be available in electronic books. For more information about Wiley
products, visit our web site at www.wiley.com.

Library of Congress Cataloging-in-Publication Data:
Sue, Marsha Petrie.
 The reactor factor : how to handle difficult work situations without going nuclear / by
Marsha Petrie Sue.
    p. cm.
 Includes bibliographical references and index.
 ISBN 978-0-470-49006-8 (cloth)
 1. Conflict management.   2. Interpersonal relations.   3. Interpersonal conflict.   I. Title.
HD42.S837 2010
 650.1–dc22
 2009016542
Printed in the United States of America.

10 9 8 7 6 5 4 3 2 1

MID-CONTINENT PUBLIC LIBRARY

3 0000 13163919 1

MID-CONTINENT PUBLIC LIBRARY
Kearney Branch
100 S. Platte-Clay Way
Kearney, MO 64060

KE

To all the people in the workforce who are struggling to be
successful but aren't quite sure what to do.

Contents

Contents

Preface

There is no topic sacred in this book because my goal is to provide a workbook for responding instead of reacting. I recommend reading the contents and choosing the topics that are important to you, right now.

- Do you want to know how obesity affects your job? It's here.
- Want to get rid of the entitlement attitude? It's here.
- How about working with the spoiled brats in your office? It's here.
- Boggled about how to handle office politics, and the grapevine? It's here.
- Are you in a state of anxiety when asked to do a presentation? It's here.
- What if you are laid off and need to find a job? It's here.
- Need to get a grip on social networks? It's here.
- Want to better manage the time you spend in meetings? It's here.
- Confused about dress codes and what to wear? It's here.

I've conducted more than 45 interviews with professionals of small and large businesses. These businesspeople provide insight to what can work and what can help you through some of the negatives in today's business world. Todd Davis, the guy who gives out his social security number in all the LifeLock ads, shares incredible insights into excellence. Gary and Judy Sitton, successful entrepreneurs who took an idea and turned it into a multi-million dollar business, give you tips on how to succeed. Add to that formula all the other people who so graciously gave me their time so I could provide insights in this book for you.

Learn to take personal responsibility so you can be free from being a job slave. You will be able to break the shackles, even if you can't afford to quit. Freedom of choice is yours if you so choose—and you do have choices.

For those of you familiar with my stuff, *The CEO of YOU: Leading Yourself to Success* shared my personal and work experiences while *Toxic People: Decontaminate Difficult People at Work Without Using Weapons or Duct Tape* is the ultimate resource for dealing with jerks at work. *The Reactor Factor* looks at what is actually happening in your world of work today and gives you the tools needed to succeed. You will find worksheets and challenges throughout.

Please check the web site at www.MarshaPetrieSue.com if you need any of the worksheets as printable documents. My hope is that you will use them for yourself, but also with people you work with. Whether you are in charge or not, the challenge remains how you improve your environment not only at work but also at home. How about involving your partner and kids in becoming more capable in handling the negatives in life?

Remember, you are in charge, and success is totally up to you.
So get busy.

—*Marsha*

If you can't do something nice, just do something. But don't sit there like a lump.

—*Dorothy L. Petrie*

Acknowledgments

Thanks to Larry Winget for introducing me to Matt Holt at John Wiley & Sons, Inc. This is my second book with Matt and his team, and they continue to give me the feedback I need, the editing to make the book readable, and the total support for success. There are so many people to mention at John Wiley, including the incredible talents of Lauren Lynch, Christine Moore, and Kate Lindsay.

But even before my introduction to the folks at John Wiley, Larry coached me, tore my materials apart, and jolted me into the realism of what it would take to tell my story and why it is so important to dump the fluff. Larry's wife Rose Mary has been an instrumental influence in keeping my life in balance with outings to golf, the spa, eating tamales, and the ever so frequent wine outings.

Jan Olsen is truly my right and left arm. She has become an excellent mind reader and, as she reminds me, talent is on her job description. Marcia Snow constantly makes sure my schedule, calendar, travels, speaking, and everything else are in order. Janita Cooper is not only a wonderful friend but produces all my CDs and DVDs by using her creativity and imagination to make me look good. Sounding and looking good is thankfully in the hands of Rocky Heyer who works with Janita at Master Duplicating.

Acknowledgments

And, of course, my now retired husband, Al. Without his believing in me and his constant encouragement I would still be hanging out in the corporate world. He knows when to leave me alone, and when I need a hug. He is the light of my life and is the best husband and partner anyone could ask for. I'm glad I married the boy named Sue.

A true friend is someone who thinks that you are a good egg even though he knows that you are slightly cracked.

—Bernard Meltzer, *radio host*

Introduction

I watched my dad, Marshall Petrie, take personal responsibility for his life and success by always seeking out new opportunities. Born in Chicago, his mother passed away upon the birth of his youngest brother, forcing my dad to grow up quickly under the direction of close relatives.

As the story goes, Marshall was a Zoot Suiter, a word meaning a male gangster, wearing the pin-striped suits, usually with baggy pants with "pegged" legs and suit jackets with wide shoulders and wide brim hats. His father, a strict German and an accountant by trade, swiftly expelled Dad from the house.

Opportunity #1—With no place to go, Dad moved to Vallejo, California, and was a bootlegger, which was a unique response to prohibition. He and his buddies would make bathtub gin, fill empty liquor bottles with the swill, and then take gunnysacks and drag them through the seawater and sand to give them the appearance of being imported. This was during prohibition, so there were sporadic visits to the local jail for their illegal deeds and bootlegging.

Opportunity #2—The bootlegger occupation wasn't working out too well so Dad became a barber, but quickly realized there was no money to be made.

Opportunity #3—In 1933, the end of prohibition, Marshall was visiting his favorite watering hole and realized that the bartender was mixing a drink the same way he had learned to whip up the foam for a shave. So his next career move was to bartending. He was gregarious and a wonderful conversationalist so he made many friends and built solid relationships.

Opportunity #4—Ten years later, the withholding tax on wages was introduced in 1943 and was instrumental in increasing the number of taxpayers to 60 million and tax collections to $43 billion. Dad saw the opportunity to provide a service helping people complete their tax forms. So the offices of Marshall Petrie, Public Accountant, were formally opened in San Pedro, California. Many of his bar patrons followed him to his new occupation. After additional studies, Dad was grandfathered to the status of Certified Public Accountant.

During my high school years, my mother, Dorothy Petrie, went back to school at the age of 50 and became a real estate broker. She leveraged all the experience and years working for my father and became a very successful Realtor and property manager. She responded well to the life of a divorced woman.

Because of my mom and dad, Dorothy and Marshall, I have transitioned my life and success. There have been many times in my career and personal life when I have made dumb decisions—and plenty of them! Additionally, there have been many opportunities lost because I decided to keep my head in the sand. Perhaps a lot like you. But I have now learned how to respond positively to negative situations at work without going nuclear and am living the Reactor Factor.

The only two helping hands you will ever have are attached to the end of your arms. Use them and stop waiting for someone to rescue you. They're not coming.

—*F. Marshall Petrie*

CHAPTER 1

Deciding to Decide

⋯

Take It, Leave It, Change It

Today's decisions are tomorrow's realities.

—Anonymous

*T*he Reactor Factor is all about making decisions to get better outcomes. I believe you always have three choices: you can (1) Take it, (2) Leave it, or (3) Change it. I call this the "TLC" of decision making. When you are stuck, you need to stop, decide to decide, and ask yourself the TLC of deciding to decide. Excuses and whining don't allow you to take a fresh look at what you can control; TLC does. TLC requires you to take personal responsibility and be accountable for your actions. True business success is established by conquering the Reactor Factor and learning how to quickly turn the negatives into more palpable and positive outcomes.

Oh, I know; life is hard, and it is not always fair. But look at it this way: you can choose to let your situation suck the life out of you; or you can rise above all the negative chatter about not being able to control your boss, your company, your peers, your subordinates, your job, your time, and your projects. And yes, it really is your choice.

In fact, every situation you face gives you the opportunity to choose and control the outcome. It stuns me that so many professionals choose *not* to take personal responsibility for their outcomes. For many, pointing fingers is easier; and then they wonder why they feel so out of control. This book will not only help you make better choices, it will also help you understand what you can control.

> *Destiny is no matter of chance. It is a matter of choice: It is not a thing to be waited for, it is a thing to be achieved.*
>
> —*William Jennings Bryan, American politician and orator*

For example, let's suppose that you are a member of a successful industry and are drawing a decent paycheck. The company has a moderate level of growth, but is always looking for ways to cut corners and save money. Your success has been moderate, and looking back, you know you have survived a few rough patches. You can learn to control the uncontrollable by focusing on these questions and more.

- Do you choose to broaden your scope and learn something new, or are you stuck in intellectual arrogance?
- Do you know your real value in the industry, or merely within your company?
- Are you prepared if the market changes—whether good or bad?

Don't get sucked into trying to control elements of business that you *can't* control. Think about the situations you face. What are you deciding to do? Are you trying to control the uncontrollable? Here are the facts:

- If you have a toxic boss, you will never change him or her.
- If a colleague is a jerk, you won't get him or her to leave.
- If you hate your job, doing nothing will not make it better.
- If the younger generation entering your business works differently than you do, you won't get them to change.
- If you are fearful of anything, take a hard look at where the fear originates.
- If you don't make enough money, complaining will not increase your pay.
- If you are overworked, taking a day off won't reduce your workload.
- If you have unpaid bills, borrowing more will not reduce your debt.

Some choices we live not only once but a thousand times over, remembering them for the rest of our lives.

—*Richard Bach, American writer*

You need to consider these factors and decide to Take It, Leave It, or Change It.

Take It

Accept the above situations for what they are, and don't let these issues throw you off balance or create stress. It is what it is; in the moment, you know that you need to do something. However, the situation isn't going to change overnight. You may decide to trigger your thinking into action by beginning to work out a plan to make the future better and different. But right now—in this very instant— you have decided to take it as it is, and not complain to anyone about your circumstance. Because, to be honest, they really don't care.

Choice: You've decided you don't like your job. You are ticked off, fed up, and are tempted to quit on the spot. You step back from the situation and realize that while leaving right away is probably not feasible, it is ultimately what you will do. You decide to make the best of it and refuse to be part of the grapevine and gossip. You will do your job to the best of your ability, including asking clarifying questions to stay on track. You start to make a plan so you know tomorrow will be better and different than today. Tomorrow might be a week, a month, a year—or even years! But right now, you will take it.

You have decided to take it, so your assertiveness is stronger than ever, and both your internal and external communications are controlled. You are managing your stress, and you're not making yourself crazy over the situation. Perhaps you just don't want to take the time right now to really tackle the event, but you have assured yourself that you will rehash the situation within three months.

Leave It

You walk away from the situation and reject it totally. You know you have to do this to save your sanity. You've had to quit a personal relationship or fire a friend or partner in your life; and you acknowledge that this will bring some emotional pain and stress. But ultimately, you move yourself away from the situation. This is the most difficult of all the choices because you are realigning into the unknown and expanding your comfort zone. You recognize that there is a risk to moving beyond where you are right now, but you are ready to face the fear of making the decision to jettison yourself to something totally new.

Choice: You are beyond being able to rationally stay, and are ready to leave skid marks and move on. Though it is high risk, you have done your planning and have a firm commitment from another employer. This position seems to be a better, if not a perfect, fit. Your gut is telling you to jump, take a risk, and go for it. You step back from it all and ask yourself, "What's the worst thing that can happen?" The answer is simple. If you don't like this new position, you can dive right back into the talent pool and start searching again. You feel good with your decision and have the confidence to jump ship.

For what is the best choice for each individual is the highest it is possible for him to achieve.

—*Aristotle, Ancient Greek philosopher*

Change It

Your boss and your job are creating stress and unrest for you. The company is exactly where you want to establish your career, but you are working with idiots. However, you decide to stay and make the best of it by changing your approach. You read up on how to handle toxic people and destructive situations, and after analyzing your own, you have new approaches through your enhanced skills. In addition, you find an internal mentor who will help you succeed, and, per his or her suggestion, you pay careful attention to the press releases and grapevine to see if any new opportunities arise for you within the company. Reviewing your education and knowledge bank, you decide to take a class that will give you tools to help you fit into the company growth. In addition, you freshen up your resume and are ready at a moment's notice when your dream position opens.

There is nothing wrong with change, if it is in the right direction.

—*Winston Churchill, British orator*

Change it: Your job is not delivering the satisfaction, challenge, or success that you want out of your career. Interviewing other segments of the business and industry seems to be a viable alternative. So you begin networking internally, externally, and through the social networks to determine what is available. Your goal is to repackage your current talents and skills and apply them to a job description that will deliver what you need. You are willing to learn and to take the risk.

You evaluate the people with whom you spend time and go to lunch and decide that they are negative and promote some of your unrest. You tell them that your break time will be study time. Gradually, you will be able to choose new break buddies and create a more positive environment at work. You are comfortable in your own skin, and you're not worried about what others will say about you.

Todd Davis, Chief Executive Officer at LifeLock, is the gentleman you see in the LifeLock advertisements that gives out his social security number. I asked him about this decision, and yes, it was his idea to spread this otherwise "secret" number, and he had a wonderful response. Davis said, "I want to be disruptive and do things that no one else will do or has thought of." He continued by saying, "And that is what I expect of everyone at LifeLock." He also said he suffers from *Blissful Ignorance* and this helps him take risks where others wouldn't.

As a leader, he lives this quote. For example, the call center employees receive full benefits from the beginning of being hired and they make one third more than the national average of CSRs (customer service representatives). This attitude has permeated the culture as well. One of LifeLock's employees had a family crisis during the holidays. Their finances were strained, so the day the employees received their holiday gift cards from the company, they quickly pooled them and presented them to a very surprised family. That is living Davis's quote and sustaining the culture, *Do what you should, not what you can*. And another example of the company's goodwill is to provide company equity to each of the more than 400 employees.

Davis expects all employees to make decisions and move fast. All he wants to know is why you did it and he'll "watch your back." Davis expects upfront communication before the chaos hits and always wants people to ask themselves, "Am I bringing value here?" Along with that statement he added that he expects to be able to ask anyone, anytime, "What are you doing and how does it contribute to the mission?" He also said, "Don't fake it here, because you will get found out!" and these people get "pruned," not fired.

He ended our interview by saying, "I owe the company my best."

LESSON

Do what you should. Not what you can.

　　Choice: Your industry has been doing well. The upturns in the economy had provided several years of sizeable bonus checks. Because you are well versed on the economy, you understand that it is cyclical and that there could be—and probably would be— a downturn. However, the money is great in your position so you decide to ride the wave as long as possible. You couldn't leave—the pay was too good! Then one day it happened and the bottom seemed to drop out of everything to do with business. The sudden cutbacks were unexpected, and you were laid off with no warning. However, your flexibility saved the day. You understood your talents, had an updated resume, and you immediately applied to other viable businesses. The list was long and included franchise companies, law firms, health-care facilities, and more.

Question: Could you truly say you fit all the criteria to work at LifeLock? Are you willing to make disruptive decisions to help your company and yourself succeed?

LESSON

Make disruptive decisions and stay on task.

How is *your* industry doing? Since the beginning of 2007, more than 70,500 workers have lost their jobs at mortgage lending institutions, according to recent company layoff announcements and data compiled by global outplacement firm Challenger, Gray & Christmas and also information from MortgageDaily.com publisher Sam Garcia. How many people working in this industry even understood the cycle and planned for it? Not many.

Meanwhile, construction companies have announced nearly 1,470,000 jobs cuts last year according to McGraw Hill Construction's "Outlook '09, Spring Update" report, while the National Association of Realtors expects membership rolls to decline this year for the first time in a decade. If business is cyclical, why were so many people shocked by these events? If the writing on the wall started in January 2007, why weren't more people prepared to face unemployment? It is your personal responsibility to prepare for the best- and the worst-case scenarios. *The Reactor Factor* is all about being prepared.

Many, probably most, housing industry employees never planned for a downturn and thought they could ride the wave of the fat paychecks forever. How do you process this industry downturn information? Microsoft is also slashing jobs as sales of PCs plummet. Employees have arrived at the stark realization that the slump in sales could last a long time, perhaps years. Think about what this will do to semiconductor chipmaker Intel, and the hundreds—maybe thousands—of vendors related to the computing industry. Technology spending will decline 3 percent, or $1.66 billion, globally this year—the first such decline in seven years—as businesses and governments cut back on their spending amid deepening recession, according to a new prediction by Forrester Research.

And how about banking? The U.S. financial industry has been shedding jobs at a record clip, and some analysts predict the pace will only accelerate over the next year and a half as banks cut costs in the face of the housing market slump and the weak economy. Analysts at financial research firm Celent said that they expect the U.S. commercial banking industry—essentially, all companies that lend or collect deposits—to lose 200,000 of its 2 million jobs.

Dave Matthews is President of Reliance Loan Center in Arizona. He says:

> I am trying to stay light on my feet, so I can react quickly if something goes wrong. We have managed to stay lean and mean, but I am implementing more and more monitoring of our customer base so we can react quickly if things change.
>
> What might change in my industry? One of my customer's largest customers files bankruptcy . . . a tenant asks for a reduction in the lease rate . . . suppliers start dragging out making their A/P payments . . . there are any number of things. The quicker I can respond, the quicker I can protect my asset (loan) and the quicker I can protect my client's deposits!

LESSON

Stay lean and mean and focus on your customer.

The following questions are critical for you to ask yourself. The questions and answers will help you make better choices when faced with negative situations. You will have critical thinking tools that will help you move to more positive and powerful results. Each of these tools is discussed in detail throughout the book.

My goal is to get you thinking about what you need to ponder and how you can Plan to Prosper. Your career does not have to be a life sentence; you do not have to feel trapped and unfulfilled. *The Reactor Factor* gives you renewed focus and strength to create the life and career you want. Write your answer after each of the following seven questions. If you want a copy of this planning sheet, check the web site at www.MarshaPetrieSue.com.

1. How is your industry doing? Good or bad?
2. When was the last time you went on the web site and read company press releases?
3. Did you read the company's annual report if you work for a public company?
4. Do you plan regular meetings with your leader to find out his or her perspective of the company and of you?
5. Do you independently determine the skills needed to make you indispensable?
6. Are you constantly polishing your skills to be a better person and employee?
7. Do you hold yourself accountable for every decision, outcome, success, and failure you have on your job?

A large component of deciding to decide is to begin with information. And that means that the choice of accepting and keeping a position is yours. No one holds a gun to your head; well, unless you are incarcerated perhaps. But more likely than not, the decision to work in a particular industry or study in a particular field is 100 percent your choice. So if you make that choice to take a job, make the decision to make the best of it. Your boss hired you to succeed, not to fail.

Like the housing, banking, and the stock market, many industries are cyclical and experience downturns every 7 to 10 years. So why don't most people plan for this day? Is it because of the money? Is it laziness or greed? Are you caught in this trap?

Some people stay in jobs they hate and continue to work for jerks. Why? It is easier not to take personal responsibility for their outcomes, and to just stay and whine. They have no clue that they *do* rule their world. They decide not to decide! How about you? Many people have a tremendous fear of change. Truth be known, we all want it just like it has always been, only better. Sorry, but better rarely involves the way it has always been. I believe that this is because fear comes with blame, and people don't want to be blamed for making a difficult or bad choice. The easy way out is to fall back on the "coulda, woulda, shoulda" scenario.

> *The best day of your life is the one on which you decide your life is your own. No apologies or excuses. No one to lean on, rely on, or blame. The gift is yours—it is an amazing journey—and you alone are responsible for the quality of it. This is the day your life really begins.*
>
> —*Bob Moawad, author*

Consider the following scenario:

Your boss, Jim, is a poor leader and always has been. As the tension in the company worsens due to the unstable economy, Jim's communication to you and the team is at an all-time low. You feel like you are floundering in turbulent seas and there is no one to rescue you. Projects are missing the deadlines and are typically overdue because of factors both inside and outside your control. You are frustrated and dread walking into the portals of the company every morning.

Take It

The situation is intolerable and continues to degrade. The good people are leaving because of Jim's terrible leadership, and even his boss doesn't know what to do with him. You plan to keep your ear to the ground, and you know you will post for a new position within the company. You hope to move to another, saner area of the firm. You have promised yourself to keep your focus on your job, and not get tied up in all the office chatter. You choose to take it, and simply do your job to the best of your ability.

Leave It

You are ready to quit, and have updated your resume. You used a recent template from the Internet, visited sites like Jobing.com and Monster.com, and determined where your skills are best positioned. You're comfortable with the idea of leaving the industry, and you have already given yourself permission to move beyond your comfort zone. You decide to hand in your resignation.

Change It

You stretch your flexibility to manage your situation. The market is tight, and you are having a hard time convincing yourself to leave. You locate a download audio file through a Google search on how to deal with difficult people. The file gives you fresh approaches with Jim. You decide to change the situation by polishing your communications and your capability to deal with difficult people. You know that you must do everything to resolve your position. You pledge to yourself to be resilient and to take a new stance. You hone your listening skills, and you pay attention to every piece of information without adding to the emotion at hand.

> *Life is great. But without bad times, we wouldn't know the difference.*
>
> —*Kermit the Frog,* Before You Leap

After you decide which choice you will make, you step back and ask yourself this question: "So what's my plan?" This is where the action starts. The strategy for each of the three choices—the TLCs—are where you decide what you will do now that the decision is made. Deciding to take it can create stress and mental havoc; leaving it means you are in a tentative job market; changing it is probably the soundest choice right now. But that's just my humble opinion.

Deciding to decide is not a spectator sport. It is like setting a goal or making a New Year's resolution, then stepping back and waiting for it to happen. I've done it, and you've done it; and at the end of the year you look back at those resolutions and realize that nothing has changed. It seems crazy to say, but I will anyway: when you decide to decide, you also have to decide to take action.

Use the worksheet in Figure 1.1 to help you move forward. Included are some issues to consider, but you need to add the issues and problems that will help you control more in your work and life. You get *your* turn in Figure 1.2.

Deciding to Decide

Issue	Take it	Leave it	Change it	What's your plan?
Discuss a pay increase	Stay where you are and don't make waves. When the industry improves, ask for a raise.	Pledge to yourself that within a month you will have your raise or quit.	Learn the best approach and practice. Keep a log of what you do and of your successes.	
Ask boss for higher level assignments	Wait and see if they notice you and give you the work.	Look for a new position that has the kinds of projects you enjoy.	Learn new skills that are needed for the top assignments.	
Boss manages poorly	Listen to others and determine if it is really the boss or you.	Find a new position.	Communicate with the boss offering candid and helpful advice.	
You manage poorly	Wait until someone tells you that you need to change, but stay aware of your management style.	Step down from your management position.	Tell your group you are working on a development plan and ask for their help.	
Your colleague has body odor	Buy a fan and room deodorizer. Leave a bar of soap on their desk.	Ask to have your desk moved.	Ask graciously if you can discuss a sensitive issue with them.	

Figure 1.1   Issues Worksheet

Issue	Take it	Leave it	Change it	What's your plan?

Figure 1.2   Blank Worksheet

It's All About Them

Helping *other* people make better decisions will actually help you create the environment that breeds successful outcomes. People who bemoan most everything and those who have become victims of circumstance can suck the life out of any team or person. Learn to turn the TLC into an external communication tool. When they approach you, simply keep the focus on what you know works—and assertively communicate.

You know what I learned? I learned that I always have three choices. I can take it—which means that I'll work on not being stressed, because I *do* have a plan and realize that tomorrow will be better and different than today. The second choice I have is to leave it—which I find to be the most difficult choice, because it takes me to a place I've never been. I have to reject where I am, and jump out of my comfort zone. But it *is* a choice.

16

The third choice I have is to change it. I have to look at my flexibility and willingness to learn a new approach. I find that usually this is the best choice, because I can rely on the skills I have or can polish them to move forward in a very positive fashion.

I call this the TLC of deciding to decide. What's *your* plan? Put the ball back in the other person's court, instead of buying into his or her misery.

Ever tried. Ever failed. No matter. Try again. Fail again. Fail Better.

—Samuel Beckett, playwright

Deciding to decide is a mindset and a technique to help you move from the terrible loop of inactivity, negativity, resentment, and anger. Focusing on the possibilities and what, realistically, you can change is the cornerstone to living the Reactor Factor.

CHAPTER 2

Spoiled Brats

▪▪▪

Entitlement, Blame, Accountability

No, I'm not talking about German sausage gone bad. A spoiled brat, as defined by the dictionary, "is a child that has been spoiled by his or her parents" (en.wikipedia.org/wiki/Spoiled_brat). Psychologists may describe spoiled children as "overindulged, grandiose, narcissistic," and even "egocentric-regressed." But this definition applies to people who are well past their "growing" years. There are countless spoiled brats in the workplace today—people who are steeped in the attitude of entitlement. They feel that the business or job they are in "owes" them for one reason or another. But you can't respond to difficult business situations if you are acting like a spoiled brat or a victim of circumstance.

Many people have fallen prey to this behavioral tendency. Some blame it on generational differences; others claim that it's the result of society gone soft; and still others declare that there is a disappearance of the work ethic. Truly, it is a combination of all of these. Layer "entitlement attitude" on top of that, and you will be sucked into the vacuum of the spoiled brat.

Consider the following statements, and use them to determine whether you've begun to develop any sense of privilege yourself; that is, if you've begun to believe that your business, colleagues, and employers "owe" you certain things.

Entitlement Detector

- ☐ I expect fairness from others.
- ☐ My good work should be recognized from my boss with a thank you.
- ☐ When I respect others, they should respect me.
- ☐ Good service should always be expected in a restaurant.
- ☐ If I perform well on my job, I should be rewarded with a raise.
- ☐ When I cover for someone at work, they should do the same for me.
- ☐ I am entitled to "life, liberty, and the pursuit of happiness."
- ☐ Others should recognize when I'm upset with a situation.
- ☐ I expect to be included in the appropriate meetings.
- ☐ My company should pay for my education and training.
- ☐ I work hard. I deserve a good life.
- ☐ People stress me out when they are incompetent.

If you answered "Yes" to any of these statements, you are probably carrying around a lot of internal anger—because people do not give you what you feel you're entitled to. If this is the case, you need to learn the subtle art of *responding*, not *reacting*. You are not "owed" anything by anyone. Instead, your challenge is to do things for people because it's healthy or mature or "right," not because you can earn "brownie points" that you can cash in whenever you want.

A life directed chiefly toward the fulfillment of personal desires will sooner or later always lead to bitterness.

—*Albert Einstein, physicist*

Who's to Blame?

Companies and employers can blame themselves for bringing out this kind of behavior in their staff, because:

- They have not set clear connections between job performance and compensation.
- All employees are rewarded in the same way, despite the quality of work that they've done.
- Automatic raises are given based on tenure rather than performance.
- Companies have poor or inconsistent communication.
- Come-and-go-as-you-please work schedules are acceptable.
- Dress codes are not enforced.
- Annual raises of 10 percent to 20 percent of base salary are automatic.
- Regular grants of stock options are expected.
- Full-coverage health insurance benefits are expected by employees.

- Consequences of poor behavior are not immediately addressed.
- Employer-subsidized soft drinks, bagels, coffee, and more are expected.

Before W. Gary Sitton, PhD, retired, he was President of Sun-Gard Bi-Tech. He developed 22 axioms and one "lesson" for business over the course of the 20-plus years he ran a software company, which was founded April 3, 1981, and run from his home for eight years. When the employee count reached 18, the company was moved to a "real office" building at the Chico Municipal Airport, California. When Gary retired in 2000, the company had more than 200 employees, revenues of $30 million a year, the lowest employee turnover rate in the industry—and the company had never been involved in litigation of any kind.

The following are Sitton's Axioms. His ideas eliminate any Spoiled Brat attitudes before they start, and he confirmed that!

Axiom #1: Make more coffee when you leave less than a full cup in the pot.

Axiom #2: The first six people you hire will set the work, social, ethical, and intellectual character of your company. Be extremely careful with these hires.

Axiom #3: Understand, respect, trust, and celebrate what employees do for you.

Axiom #4: Be honest with your employees, even when it hurts.

Axiom #5: Never borrow money.

Axiom #6: Don't confuse being smart with having a knack for something.

Axiom #7: Encourage employees with a negative attitude to work for competitors.

Axiom #8: Let employees make important decisions and mistakes (after all, *you* got to do both).

Axiom #9: Hire a few people that tease and cut up (they keep things light).

Axiom #10: Listen carefully to your clients, they will tell you how to stay in business.

Axiom #11: Leave your office door unlocked and open.

Axiom #12: Minimize company policy and procedures.

Axiom #13: Honor all contracts.

Axiom #14: Under-commit and over-deliver.

Axiom #15: Family comes first; work comes second.

Axiom #16: The best committee size is one.

Axiom #17: Get paid for your work.

Axiom #18: Take time to chat with employees.

Axiom #19: Anyone can be replaced.

Axiom #20: Don't let attorneys tell you how to run your business.

Axiom #21: Employee turnover is much more expensive than paying well.

Axiom #22: Never, ever think you have figured out how to run a successful business.

LESSON

The most important thing you can do for your clients is *stay in business*.

I recently spoke to mortgage brokers and loan officers about personal responsibility, increasing sales, and success. The president of one company agreed with an analogy I had been told by another industry leader. The group was whining and certainly displaying difficult behavior—and so he chimed back with this:

"So when your numbers are terrific—is it because you are such a fabulous sales person and so good at your job? And when the bottom fell out of the real estate market and many of the financial markets, was it the economy's fault for your numbers tanking? Then why did 20 percent of the team continue to make their numbers and succeed?" There was silence in the room. His point was well taken.

My belief is that a certain percentage of people have learned to be resilient in their jobs and consciously make the decision not to be spoiled brats. The toxic behavior of a whine and cheesier is easy to adopt (read *Toxic People: Decontaminate Difficult People at Work Without Using Weapons or Duct Tape*), and is reserved for the lazy few who don't take the time to figure out what *does* work—and what they should leave behind.

So, what's *your* perspective? Do you fall into the Spoiled Brat frame of mind; or have you figured out how to pull yourself up and move forward no matter what?

Spoiled Brats

To hold the same views at forty as we held at twenty is to have been stupefied for a score of years, and take rank, not as a prophet, but as a non-teachable brat, well birched and none the wiser.

— *Robert Louis Stevenson, writer and poet*

Remember Italian economist Vilfredo Pareto's 80/20 rule? In essence, it states that, for many events, roughly 80 percent of the effects come from 20 percent of the causes. I personally think that this is why 20 percent of the investors today are investing in the financial markets—and 80 percent are whining because they overextended themselves, and oftentimes, because of their greed!

Employees expect to receive all of the benefits mentioned above based solely on the fact that they are on the payroll. However, most companies have neglected to make a connection between benefits, perks, or other extras and the company's financial performance—or even the employees' performance. So, instead of stimulating productivity and loyalty, the company's crowd-pleasing and costly benefits, bonuses, and perks are simply taken for granted. Employees have become spoiled brats. And leaders don't know how to lead this new mentality.

If you are employed in this kind of situation, it is your responsibility to get the details and pull yourself out of the "entitlement spiral." It is your job to snap out of it and value what you are receiving. That's what personal responsibility is all about.

So where does entitlement come from? The phenomenon of employee entitlement can be traced to a faulty "psychological contract" between an organization and the employees. This implies an understanding on the part of employees about what they contribute to the organization, and what they expect from it in return.

Personally, I believe that responsibility and accountability are interchangeable. The terms are defined as follows:

Responsibility

▮ The state or fact of having a duty to deal with something, or of having control over someone.
▮ The state or fact of being accountable or to blame for something.
▮ The opportunity or ability to act independently and make decisions without authorization.

Accountability

The action(s) of a person, organization, or institution required or expected to justify decisions; responsible

When you think about the difference between responsibility and accountability, there really doesn't seem of be much of a difference.

There are two primary choices in life: to accept conditions as they exist, or accept the responsibility for changing them.

—*Denis Waitley, American motivational speaker and author*

Leadership Choices

In the coaching side of my business, I am often amazed at the attitudes that some employees display. Apparently, some people just don't pay attention to controlling what is important and letting go of the rest. Here is one of my favorite examples.

I work with a health-care company that is still growing and expanding at a record pace, despite the downturns of the economy. Company CEO Pete asked me to have a joint meeting with his assistant. Because of the dynamic evolution of his region, Pete understood the need to have a strong support person. His schedule is bulging with high-level meetings, intense negotiations, and hiring the best doctors. He must be able to rely on his assistant for tasks such as:

■ Mining through e-mail.
■ Being a gatekeeper for phone calls.
■ Beginning his day with the top priorities.
■ Helping him find more time by taking responsibility for some of the mundane chores of running his life.
■ Answering calls in an expeditious manner.
■ Scheduling calls, appointments, and travel.
■ Confirming all details on potential doctors' travel details.
■ Working with the business development specialists to make sure their needs are met.
■ Being his eyes and ears in the office.

His current assistant, Gretchen, and I sat down with Pete to determine what was needed to manage his day. Unfortunately, Gretchen's attitude and unpleasant demeanor was apparent even before the meeting started. Pete shared with her his epiphany and the "ah-ha" moment he had experienced from completing an audio book on leadership, *Execution: The Discipline of Getting Things Done* by Larry Bossidy. The message for leaders was to evaluate and insist on the appropriate support. Pete was specific, gracious, and detailed. Pete then asked that I have a conversation with Gretchen to determine the best approach for her to meet his needs, and see what I could provide in coaching her to success.

When Pete left the room, Gretchen launched into a tirade about how she had been lied to by her boss. One of the spoiled brat comments she made that permeated the rest of the conversation was: "One year ago, Pete promised me the office manager position; and he lied to me, because he didn't promote me." I replied with a question for her: "What kind of process or check-off list did you come up with to review with Pete so you knew you were on track for the promotion?" Gretchen informed me, "It's not my job. He should have done this and didn't. See how he lies to me?"

We continued our conversation, and I reminded her that *she* was the one who had to take personal responsibility for her career and current job. We left it at this: Gretchen would think about staying with the company and in two weeks would have a decision. If she needed to talk, I would be available. The entire time she was relaying this, she also revealed to me that she wanted to be a lawyer and work in an industry where she "wouldn't have to put up with people like Pete." Really? I don't think that's how it would work out. At that point, Gretchen doubted if she would make that kind of career move. But hopefully—in whatever industry she chooses—Gretchen will be welcomed to the real world shortly, and will quickly realize that the spoiled brat attitude is not well accepted, particularly in this employee shoppers' market.

Gretchen's position perfectly depicts the kind of spoiled and entitlement behavior that pervades business today. Did she notice the layoffs that are currently occurring around the world? Is she so self-centered that she doesn't realize that Pete can take his re-quirements list into a market place that's swimming with high-level assistants looking for *any* job? Has Gretchen not checked the pay scale to see how she ranks with other similar positions in the area? In my opinion, there was not a hint of realism accepted, particularly in this employee market.

> *When a milestone is conquered, the subtle erosion called entitlement begins its consuming grind. The team regards its greatness as a trait and a right. Halfhearted effort becomes habit and saps a champion.*

> *—Pat Riley, professional basketball coach*

Randy Luebke, RMA, RFC, is a retirement specialist at Nations Home Funding. He was kind enough to write the following de-scription of how he is handling an otherwise devastating market. He continues to make the choice of flexibility versus whining and becoming a victim to something he can't control:

> *The mortgage industry went into a recession in August 2007. Now, nearly 75 percent of the employees in our industry have left. That's triple the unemployment during the great depression. My feeling is: good. Why? Because like most businesses that find themselves thriving, they attract those who just want to make a quick buck and truly don't understand the long-term implications of their actions. Now it's time for those people to go away. Far away!!!*

> *Did I respond? It's kind of like contracting a terminal disease. First it's denial. Then it's anger. Then it's resignation. Then is GOYA (Get Off Your Anatomy). I'm one of those people who always see opportunity in adversity. For example, I cut my staff to the bone. What a blessing that was to discover all the slop in my systems and that all the work I thought was being done had been swept under the rug.*

Next, you realize that you really can't do everything and working 24/7 is not a viable option, so I've become much better at deciding what I should do. Someone once told me that if you manage your minutes that the hours, days, weeks, months, and years will take care of themselves. So true!

Today my motto is simplify, act, document. Simplify everything I do, always looking for ways to eliminate the unnecessary and accomplish more by doing less. Act on my decisions now. Planning is valuable. Acting on your plans: priceless. Finally, I'm documenting all my processes because I know that I will staff-up again and I want to have written systems to use that I can teach others how to do what I do. Michael Gerber (E-Myth) would be so proud!

That's how I have reacted to adversity. I know that I am one who does not know how to give up and that when things change, I'd better change with them or suffer the consequences. Conversely, I also know that adversity is just opportunity that has not made itself understood yet. It's a good life!

LESSON

Change or suffer the consequences.

Step Out of the Spoiled Brat Syndrome

If you are really serious about taking control of your job as a knowledge worker and making more money, you have to take 100 percent responsibility for *everything you do*. And the first step is turning yourself and your job into a controllable business factor. You must dump any thinking about what others "owe" you. You are completely in charge of your success. However, there aren't many people in the professional world who are operating under this belief system. The following are excuses that I hear employed spoiled brats use—and some of my considerations:

- I go beyond the call of duty on my job. Instead: I use my strengths and put myself in situations that maximize them.
- They don't appreciate how hard I work. Instead: I set regular meetings to validate expected outcomes and to share my successes and failures with my superior.
- I am smarter than they think I am. Instead: Ask for challenging, high-profile assignments and projects.
- They change the process just to stir the pot. Instead: Be flexible and learn to quickly adapt to new methods.
- I don't have time for all the formalities and niceties. Instead: I know that manners and graciousness are part of success.

Feedback analysis and self-awareness will validate whether you are meeting these marks. When you start a project, keep track of the outcomes, even if they are years down the path. Two ideas:

1. Use a scorecard to validate (or invalidate) other people's perception of you. E-mail me at mps@marshapetriesue.com to receive a sample scorecard that you can customize for your environment.
2. Create a system for keeping track of your successes. An online journal. It's like your own personal blog, but you don't post it! Try this one: www.journal4ever.com/.

Is Entitlement a Generational Issue?

Many people believe it is only Generation Y that has become the Spoiled Brats. I beg to differ. The perception can be found in any of the following groups:

Born Before 1946:	Veterans	75 million working
1946–1962:	Baby Boomers	80 million working
1963–1977:	Generation X	46 million working
1978–1999:	Generation Y	76 million working

There's no question, however, that members of the most recent generation to enter the workforce *do* operate differently than most of their predecessors. In order to work amicably with Gen Y, you might try the following four ideas:

1. Tear up historical job descriptions. I mean really—people aren't doing what's written in them anyway, so there is a gap between reality and the written word. Gen Y wants the reality of the job, not some overstated litany of outdated words.
2. Become a facilitator and mentor. Dump your role as an authority. It does not work with Gen Y. Remember: their "helicopter" parents hovered, and became friends and companions to them. So they expect the same of you.

> *Generation Gap: A chasm, amorphously situated in time and space that separates those who have grown up absurd from those who will, with luck, grow up absurd.*
>
> —*Bernard Rosenberg*, Dictionary for the Disenchanged

3. Generation Y is tech-savvy, nimble, and enthusiastic, but they need structure. Spell out what the outcome needs to be and give them flexible direction.
4. Remember that members of this generation take criticism personally. The old "sandwich" approach—whereby you tell them something good, then give criticism, then end with another positive point—simply doesn't work. Remember the "serial position effect"; in other words, people remember the beginning and end.

If you want happiness for a lifetime—help the next generation.

—*Chinese Proverb*

Members of Generation Y are nothing if not opinionated, and they are more than willing to provide their two cents to co-workers and businesses alike. For example, coffee giant Starbucks *used to* sell breakfast sandwiches in 2008, which makes sense, because they sell coffee. After all, a normal routine to which many of us have adhered over the years is eating breakfast, the most important meal of the day. But did you notice the words *used to*? A group of haughty, loudmouthed critics—reportedly members of Generation Y (I will consider this the "brat" pack)—convinced Starbucks founder Howard Schultz to discontinue the breakfast fare because—as they claimed—"The egg sandwiches debased the Starbucks image because the scent of the warmed sandwiches interfered with the coffee aroma in our stores." (Well, at least Mr. Schultz is trying to make sure all the Baristas know that "breve" is the term coined by Starbucks for half-and-half by closing the stores for three hours in the recent past to make sure all were properly trained.)

Forbes magazine Editor-in-Chief Steve Forbes writes about the fallout from this decision: Starbucks stock price falling by half, leaving shareholders feeling as if they've been drinking airline coffee. Now the company is closing stores and has laid off masses of their coffee servers.

Here is the real issue: the minority starts ruling the majority because, as many know, the squeaky wheel gets greased. I even read a statistic that says that 98 percent of the customer service issues are caused by 2 percent of the people—a statistic that is even more stunning than Vilfredo Pareto's 80/20 rule. So—what does this mean? That the rest of us have to suffer, because a handful of spoiled brats are more vocal and become whiners. And other people actually *change* to address this small majority's complaints. We are then all infected with their toxic behavior.

The question is this: How do you synthesize this information into tips that you can apply personally and professionally; and how do you instill these ideas in others, whether at work or at home? Here is the personal responsibility condensed list.

Quick tips for total responsibility:

- You must assume 100 percent responsibility for your life. You are the CEO of YOU.
- Quit making excuses—they are a lazy person's way of not taking control.
- Don't react; learn to respond. Your outcomes are a result of how you learn to take action.
- Today decides tomorrow, so be careful of what you decide to do. It is 100 percent your choice.
- Quit complaining.

Spoiled Brats

Unfortunately, current media and commercials only exacerbate the Spoiled Brat syndrome. During the 1970s, McDonald's restaurants built an entire ad campaign around the slogan, "You *deserve* a break today." In the 1980s, another ad campaign said, "*Pamper* yourself with Calgon." In the 1990s, it was "You *owe* it to yourself to buy a Mercedes Benz." Society continues to bombard us with the message that we *deserve* it! Think about Queen's song, "I Want It All." A Dr. Pepper commercial featured this song, but the most problematic use of it was by Chase Bank. The message was that you deserve a huge new TV, because you have credit availability on your Chase card. How about you? Do you wonder why you have thousands of dollars racked up on your credit cards and are in debt? Do you still think you "deserve" that time off, or that new car, or that cruise?

And it doesn't seem that the message being sent to Generation Y is becoming any more realistic. Include the song from *High School Musical 3* "I Want It All" by Ashley Tisdale and you have another example of how our younger set is being permeated with this Spoiled Brat and entitlement attitude. They are sadly realizing that the land of milk and honey is souring, just as its members get their careers into full swing.

With the unemployment rate skyrocketing, employees under 30 have the most reason for worry. Joblessness is far higher among younger people than for those later in their careers. For workers under 29, the unemployment rate in 2009 jumped to more than 11 percent, compared with fewer than 9 percent a year ago, according to the U.S. Department of Labor figures. That is far worse than the overall rate of 7.2 percent, which is up from 4.9 percent a short time ago. The rate for teenage workers, from 16 to 19, is far

35

worse—approaching 20 percent. For workers in their thirties and older, the rate is still under 7 percent, and generally declines as workers get older. Solution? Step away from the entitlement attitude! Don't fall victim to the Spoiled Brat Syndrome. This is all about taking control of your life and future.

Let us not underestimate the privileges of the mediocre. As one climbs higher, life becomes ever harder; the coldness increases, responsibility increases.

—*Friedrich Nietzsche, German classical scholar*

Business today has lots of room for those great German sausages—especially when they come in a fresh kaiser roll. But I know that *no* leader has any room for spoiled brats; and these whiners will more likely than not wind up in the bread line.

You either create or allow most events that happen to you. It's that simple.

CHAPTER 3

Give Up or
Toughen Up

■■■

React or Respond?

History proves that it is easier to give up than to toughen up. Opting to give up is a reaction, whereas toughening up is a response.

Example: You lose your job. Is throwing in the towel your only option? Is everything hopeless? No matter what the economic climate, there are always opportunities. As dismal as things may seem, business isn't screeching to a complete halt. Many businesses have already figured out how to adapt. Some companies recognize and seize opportunities and they wind up with additional market share. Entrepreneurs step into the market and launch new ventures. It all starts with your state of mind and attitude. Will you react or respond?

When you choose to toughen up, you apply learning, experience, and skills to move your situation and achieve a more positive outcome. Think about this from the following health-based point of view:

Problems are to the mind what exercise is to the muscle; they toughen and make strong.

—*Norman Vincent Peale*

For example, human "reactions and responses" are often taken into account when considering medications. A patient's reaction to a prescription is negative, whereas as a response indicates that they are on the road to recovery. This definition is the cornerstone to the Reactor Factor; deciding to have a good or bad outcome is totally up to you.

The following are all important components of a given *reaction* to something:

- The reason you develop a particular reaction to a situation relates to your past experience, perception, impression, or insight to a particular event. Your genetics can even play a role.
- Most people with a drug allergy have been exposed to that drug or a similar drug prior. When a person is exposed to the drug again, the antibodies take action and set off the allergic response.
- For many, medication allergies go undetected until they take a drug and actually experience an allergic reaction.

■ The best way to avoid a medication allergy is to avoid the medication that can cause it.

The following are all important components of a given *response* to something:

■ Your behavioral "immune system" is activated in response to the situation.
■ Skills are honed and ready to use when a situation, event, or person makes you "sick."
■ You choose not to knee jerk, and know that your choice will determine the outcome.
■ Countering or even ignoring the situation may be how you choose to respond. But you make a decision not to be a jerk and to take personal responsibility, one way or the other, for the situation.

There is therefore now no adjudging guilt of wrong to them, which are in Christ Jesus, who walk not after the dictates of the flesh (practice reacting), *but after the dictates of the Spirit* (practice responding).

—Romans 8:1

Core differences between reactions and responses are illustrated in Figure 3.1.

You deal with adversity and negative situations in your own way. It's not always apparent upon observing the difference between reacting and responding to adverse events that makes the most sense. When adversity strikes and you react, it is typically an emotional retort—and one that usually does more harm than good. Viewing

React	Respond
Knee-jerk	Learned respond
Angry	Calm
Anxious	Eager
Quick fix	Considerations
I win—You lose	We collaborate
Stressed	Balanced
Retort	Ignore
Know-it-all	Asks thoughtful questions
Counter	Consider
Give up	Toughen up
Mental terrorism	Mental confidence
Catastrophic	Fortunate
Devastating	Manageable
Problem	Solution

Figure 3.1   Reactions and Responses

adversity as an attack is usually the problem, and one that stems from our past experience. In the following cases it's easy to see how someone can feel like they are being personally attacked and the possible reaction:

▌ You are blindsided by negative feedback.

Your reaction? You become angry, defensive, upset, and vengeful.

Better response: You can choose *not* to get angry by breathing, pausing, and reducing the intensity of your emotional state. Attempt to calm yourself down; this will allow you to question and dig deeper to determine the reason you received the negative comments. Take the feedback at face value.

Consider conducting a self-awareness check to see what you can learn from this feedback in terms of other people's perception of you.

∎ Your pay increase is not what you expected.

Your reaction? The boss is an idiot, and really doesn't like you. This is his vengeance! Now you'll show *him* who is boss.

Better response: You decide to set a meeting with your manager within 30 days to determine whether it is your performance, or whether the status of the company is different than you thought. You make a promise to yourself not to discuss this issue with colleagues.

∎ There is a negative rumor spinning around the office about you.

Your reaction? You immediately deny the false story and counter the gossip with one of your own.

Better response: You can ignore the rumor. Or, if you know who started it, you can ask them privately to clarify what they said. Or, you can bring it up in a public venue by saying, "It's weird to keep hearing this information about myself; because it is so untrue. Too bad the person who started it doesn't have enough guts to approach me directly. How sad is *that?*" Do express professional disappointment in this, but don't allow your emotions to drive your conversation.

∎ You lose your job without warning.

Your reaction? Typically anger, blame, pointing fingers, justifying why the layoff is wrong.

Better response: You look at this turn of events as an opportunity to reposition yourself, and perhaps chase that dream you've always had. You do not allow yourself to have a "pity party." You start getting busy on your networking to find a new position where you choose to spend your time and energy.

▮ You are verbally attacked in a public meeting.

Your reaction? Attack back, or clam up and complain about it later.

Better response: You take a deep breath to get oxygen to your brain, and calmly respond by saying, "It's interesting that you would say that. I would like to speak to you after the meeting; and I know that as a fellow professional, that is something you will do." Don't let them off the hook; make sure to set a time to meet.

Understand that each of these scenarios will undoubtedly cause some level of stress; but also remember that stress is simply your perspective that your resources are not adequate to deal with the circumstances. The more you learn, and the more skills you hone, the less stress you feel when adversity hits you. So when you are stressed out, stop and ask yourself, "What skill do I need to better manage this situation?" That helps you to develop the tools you need to respond constructively. You may even have the tool already, but just haven't used it in a while.

In fact, did you know that reading a book, listening to a tape, or watching a training video several times will actually *instill* the ideas so deeply that you will automatically be able to apply the proficiency? The problem is we have unwanted thoughts, feelings, and impulses that drive the outcomes we have. You must remain aware of the fact that *you* are the one who controls your consciousness and your subconscious. Example: When some people are outsourced, they view the event as an opportunity to take positive action in their lives. These are the people who are aware of their thought processes and how it affects their stress, and who wind up in a better position than they were in before. The Reactor Factor confirms and gives strength to these people, and guides them to experiencing better outcomes.

Never give in! Never give in! Never, never, never, never—in nothing great or small, large or petty.

—*Winston Churchill*

I continue to be amazed at the people who expect me to buy into their whining and negative focus. I just won't do it, because I know it will affect the way I think and the outcome it will have on my actions. One poor soul e-mailed me through my blog to complain about people being loud and arrogant. His question was, "Should I act like them to get noticed?" This is not rocket science; hoping I could give a little guidance, I made several suggestions. I even sent him a download from my shopping cart for free that might help him take a different approach. Did it help? NO! He continued to whine, and didn't pay attention to one word I suggested. Well, that's just too bad. He opted to be the pit in the bowl of cherries of life; it was 100 percent his choice.

The point here is that you can only help yourself respond, because other people will continue to choose to react. It is really that simple.

The greatest pleasure in life is doing what people say you cannot do.

—*Walter Bagehot, British political analyst, economist, and editor*

Kathey Dufek is the Director of Human Resources at The Doctors Company and says the following on the subject:

It's been a privilege in my work over the years to counsel employees on a myriad of issues—some small in nature and others of critical importance. Nearly all of my counseling has to do with turning a negative into a positive. For example, employees have asked me, "How can I deal with a manager who I don't get along with or who doesn't like me," or, "How do I deal with a fellow employee who talks about me behind my back?" or "I cannot work in a hostile environment any longer and have to tell someone what's going on." The answers to these questions and statements can be simple or very complex depending on the situation and the persons involved. However, in each instance I am expected to handle them professionally and as expediently as possible to resolve the issue while staying within the parameters of company policy and state or federal laws. The answers I give employees aren't always what they want to hear, but I know I've done my job well—and turned a negative into a positive—when the same employee comes to me on other issues seeking my advise because they believe that I will do the best for them that I can.

LESSON

Respond to a situation by seeking advice from professionals when needed and don't react if the answer isn't what you wanted to hear.

Picture the following scenario: A customer enters a retail store waving her receipt, obviously angry and upset. Having placed a phone order, this client had received the merchandise, but had been overcharged from the quoted price. Now, screaming in front of other patrons, the upset customer goes into great detail about how the store is trying to cheat her. Feeling very uncomfortable, the clerk—Anne—had a choice: to react or respond to this situation.

React: Anne will concentrate on her own discomfort of being the only one listening to the customer's frustration; she just wants the situation to go away. Two thoughts come to her mind:

1. She can cave in immediately and refund the entire order, giving the customer instant satisfaction.
2. She can react defensively, and blame the customer for being irrational and crazy. She can inform her that, "There's nothing I can do. You have to call customer service," in an attempt to get rid of the client.

The problem with "reacting" is that Anne is only focused on *her* narrow experience of the situation. The result? Either the store or the customer loses.

Respond: Even though Anne feels uncomfortable with an angry client, she realizes that there is something more important to keep in mind. She knows that she needs to dig deeper and ask questions to obtain more information about what went wrong in this situation. Every client is a valuable part of the store's customer base; therefore, Anne feels capable of handling it, and puts her own discomfort aside. Anne has learned to apologize to the upset client and to assure her that the situation can be quickly resolved once she provides more information. Upon receiving this information, she quickly determines that the client's order has been switched with another person, and makes the adjustment to correct the mistake.

Anne uses active coping in the second scenario—a response that promotes better mental and physical health. Don't fall into the trap of avoidance, repression, and denial. That approach only promotes unmanaged stress.

Now, what happens if you face a situation like the one mentioned above and you really don't know what to do? The first step to take is to apologize, and tell the angered person that although you aren't quite sure how to proceed, you are going to find someone who is. You only need to do this once; learning and applying is the real key here. Otherwise, you fall back into "react" mode.

As indicated in Figure 3.2, your brain spins through four different levels of thinking in order to make a decision and take action. Beginning with perception, you quickly see how your mind shoves you into action.

Perception: This is your awareness to anything that typically originates through your senses—frames of reference developed through your experience, examples, parenting, culture, gender, geography, and more. Perception is the process of attaining awareness or understanding of sensory information.

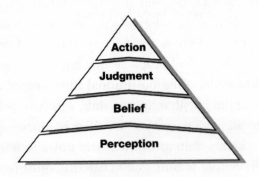

Figure 3.2   Four Levels of Thinking

What is madness? To have erroneous perceptions and to reason correctly from them.

—Voltaire, French philosopher and writer

Belief: In your view, is it true? This is what determines a "belief." It is your opinion or conviction, and a state or habit of mind—as well as the confidence in the truth or existence of something. This means there doesn't have to be "proof" that it is true. When someone learns a particular fact, it can become a belief.

A new way of thinking has become the necessary condition for responsible living and acting. If we maintain obsolete values and beliefs, a fragmented consciousness and self-centered spirit, we will continue to hold onto outdated goals and behaviors.

—Dalai Lama, head of the Dge-lugs-pa order of Tibetan Buddhists

Judgment: This describes the cognitive process of reaching a decision or drawing conclusions—the mental ability to understand and discriminate. "She has an eye for project management."

Judgment is like elastic, it snaps back at you.

—Anonymous

Action: This is the decision you make because of your perception, belief, and judgment; in other words, what you decide to "do." Action results in an outcome or the final product, end result, or consequence. It's the initiative you take to move forward and make change. Most people automatically react, because they have not learned how to respond.

Action is the antidote to despair.

—*Joan Baez, American singer and songwriter*

The different ways each of these cognitive responses are affected by reactions versus responses in the workplace can be described as follows:

React

Perception—Each employee has learned how to communicate.

Belief—They believe that they can't look uninformed in a meeting.

Judgment—They decide not to interact in the meeting.

Action—They are upset because decisions were made with which they don't agree.

Respond

Perception—Each employee has learned how to communicate.

Belief—They believe that they are skilled communicators.

Judgment—They decide to discuss their findings, information, and data.

Action—They are okay with the outcome, because their ideas were considered.

Reactions can have a significant effect on the negative aspects of life; usually they make a given situation worse. Typically reactions are impulsive and destructive, while responses are not. Example: Reacting immediately by providing answers to a situation instead of asking questions to gather more information. The solution is to build your confidence, so if there *is* any level of apprehension in your thinking, you can bolster your comfort level by saying, "I've not thought about your perspective in that way. Let me give that some thought."

Now, you might be saying to yourself: "Well—you have no idea who I'm working with!" You are right about that, but I can honestly say that if you are not comfortable with the statement you're about to make, you have set up a communication ground rule that lets the other person *expect* you to jump right in with a comment. You've set it up this way so that you can change it! And don't think this will happen overnight. You must reinforce this practice by choosing statements such as, "As I mentioned before, I would like to give this a little thought. So please bear with me, and I will have a more helpful response for you."

Matt Holt is Vice President and Publisher of John Wiley & Sons. Here's what he has to say, "I, and really Wiley in general, plan to focus on the things that we can control and keeping an eye on the things beyond our control. We're much more agile and really trying to make smart decisions. Everything revolves around: is this valuable to the customer, is it unique, are we being cost-effective, is it timely?"

Despite the dire times that we face, there is tremendous opportunity to gain market- and mind-share of our customer base. (And thanks to Matt and his staff for publishing my book!)

LESSON

Don't try to control the uncontrollable.

Your Turn

What would *you* say and do in situations like these? Well, if you don't practice your responses, you will never change the Reactor Factor. Some suggested answers to these 12 scenarios are on the web site www.MarshaPetrieSue.com under "Free Stuff."

1. Your colleague presents a project that the two of you just completed. You keep waiting for him to mention your part in the project, because you know that *you* came up with the idea for the winning solution. However, he is nearing the end of the presentation—and still hasn't said your name.

   React or respond? What action and initiative do you take?

   _____

   _____

2. As the team leader, you are responsible for ensuring that all members are prepared for the client presentation. One team-mate named Jerry is not there, and you must begin without him. Halfway through your presentation, Jerry comes racing in, makes a commotion that the client notices, and flops down without apology.

   React or respond? What action and initiative do you take?

   _____

   _____

3. The media is buzzing about the recent changes in your company—and they are not positive. You are confused, and

you have no idea how to go forward. Your boss is always in meetings, and information about the changes is not being shared.

React or respond? What action and initiative do you take?

_____

_____

4. You have an employee or colleague who constantly lies. These actions make you angry and because of your friendship, you believe that the behavior hurts your credibility and the trust others have in you.

React or respond? What action and initiative do you take?

_____

_____

5. You have a good job doing something you enjoy. The prospect of being promoted seems unlikely, but you have faith that something might change. Your competitor approaches and offers you a position, under the condition that you bring all of your current clients with you to the new company. The ethics of the situation cross your mind, but the competitor is willing to double your pay.

React or respond? What action and initiative do you take?

_____

_____

6. You keep your desk organized and neat. Because of the type of position that you are in, other people need access to your desk and supplies. You can tell when your colleague Joan has been at your work area, because she leaves everything in disarray. You have approached her, and she always responds by telling you to "cool down." You are quickly approaching the end of your rope with Joan!

   React or respond? What action and initiative do you take?

   _____

   _____

7. Danny is an important member of your team, and an excellent producer, but he comes in late and leaves early. Others are questioning you as to why he gets away with this behavior. You don't want to lose Danny as an employee, but you have to respond in some way, because the other team members have written you a fairly caustic joint letter on the topic.

   React or respond? What action and initiative do you take?

   _____

   _____

8. Your employee Bob does only what is expected of him; no more, and no less. He is always on time and never misses a day of work. However, the dynamics of your business, customers, and projects demand that you have someone who is creative and takes the initiative. Meanwhile, Bob has approached you

and asked to reduce his workload because he is overwhelmed. You don't know what to do.

React or respond? What action and initiative do you take?

_____

_____

9. You lose your job without warning with three months severance pay. Though your current company has offered assistance in finding your next position, the grapevine is telling you that this is just lip service—and that the company really doesn't care what happens to you.

React or respond? What action and initiative do you take?

_____

_____

10. Someone starts a rumor about you in the office that is not true. You know who has done it but are hesitant to approach him because you fear retribution. His actions have not always been in the best interest of the business, and you have proof of this.

React or respond? What action and initiative do you take?

_____

_____

11. Your raise is not what you expected and you are having a difficult time setting another meeting with your boss.

Other employees have already complained to her about their raises.

React or respond? What action and initiative do you take?

_____

_____

12. You get blindsided by feedback during a public meeting. You know that the other attendees are wrong, and you need to straighten this out before it gets any worse.

React or respond? What action and initiative do you take?

_____

_____

If you would like ideas with the responses to the above scenarios, please e-mail us at mps@marshapetriesue.com.

Anyone can give up, it's the easiest thing in the world to do. But to hold it together when everyone else would understand if you fell apart, that's true strength.

— *Unknown*

Norma Strange, Partner at Residual Income Technologies, one of my colleagues and friends, shared a great, real-life experience in which responding instead of reacting paid off for her big time. I had asked her, "What have you done lately that stretches your limits?" Norma's response:

I had a meeting at work where I learned that my friends—and now business partners—wanted to talk with and meet leading distributors in direct selling companies. As I left the meeting, a luxury car with a vanity plate pulled right in front of me. It was exactly who my friends wanted to meet, so I followed him as he pulled into the next parking lot. I walked up to this man and his wife and started a conversation. I told them that my friends would only be in town one more day, and asked if they'd like to meet them and sample their high-impact direct-selling training. They said yes!

Imagine if I'd been too uncomfortable to approach this stranger and ask that simple question. It was a bold move for me then, as I had never done something like that. I had always tended to hold myself back, but was glad that I had decided not to this time.

LESSON

Choose to respond to the situation, be assertive, and start a conversation.

Gwen Gallagher is President of Old Republic Home Protection and had this to say:

For us, we've found it's all about attitude! Basically, as Rosalyn Carter once said, "If you doubt you can accomplish something, then you can't accomplish it. You have to have enough confidence in your ability, and then be tough enough to follow through."

Regardless of the market, regardless of the competition, we have to have belief that we can not only maintain, but also grow. If we don't believe in ourselves, how can we get others to believe in us?

As a result of our attitudes and belief, drive and determination, we actually grew our business last year, in one of the toughest years in real estate. This year (2009), we are already surpassing last year's numbers by 20 percent and at that rate, we'll have our biggest year ever!

Hard decisions? None really. It's been more about:

- Focusing on the activities that will get us the results we wish to achieve (vital few versus trivial many)
- Evaluating and then eliminating expenses that aren't getting us closer to our goal (top and bottom line)

LESSON

Tune up your attitude.

On a Personal Note . . .

My husband, Al, is the consummate outdoorsman. When we first met, he asked me to go camping with him. I was raised with the perception that "camping" was something unappealing. My belief was that proper women didn't camp—which made my judgment of this suggestion an automatic reaction of, "Are you nuts?"

The action and initiative I chose to take was to respond—and not react. However, my husband and I agreed to maintain certain camping comforts.

- We would tent, and not sleep in the back of the truck or on the ground.

■ I would have a port-a-potty.
■ We would share the cooking and clean-up chores for meals.
■ I would purchase the appropriate clothing and shoes.
■ Al would have to put on clean underwear and socks every day.
■ I would attend a "Becoming an outdoor woman" weekend.
■ In trade, he would go to the symphony and the theater with me.

So—after more than a decade and a half—we are living happily ever after. I decided to toughen up and not wimp out.

Be who you are and say what you feel because those who mind don't matter and those who matter don't mind.

—Dr. Seuss, American writer

Know When to Cut Your Losses

Sometimes, giving up is necessary. Quitting may very well be good for your health, according to a study reported on by the Association for Psychological Science. The lesson isn't necessarily a new one: it simply states that it's helpful to know when to cut your losses. But here is the catch: the upside to the study for those less willing to give up on goals easily is that of the participants who *did* quit, those who were more willing to set and reengage in new goals had more sense of purpose. Notice they didn't give up *altogether*; they merely modified their actions to fit a new set of goals.

So the question is: Will you give up, or toughen up? The choice, as always, is yours.

CHAPTER 4

What Leaders Want

■ ■ ■

Attitude, Core Values, Outcomes

What do leaders want? They want you, the employee, manager, director, or supervisor, to take personal responsibility for all of the outcomes of your actions. It's a pretty simple request, really. However, most people do not learn what this means, or do not have the role models to help them be totally accountable for their results.

Do you have any idea why you were hired for your job, or how you will move to your next position? Do you know what your leader, shareholders, or people in power at your company want from you? My independent research found that leaders say . . .

NO to:

▮ Negative comments
▮ Arrogance and self-absorption
▮ Being withdrawn and failing to participate
▮ Lack of tact
▮ Unprofessional appearance
▮ Lack of experience
▮ Poor skill set
▮ A sense of entitlement
▮ Being unprepared and unwilling to do research

YES to:

▮ Expressing enthusiasm
▮ Taking initiative
▮ Experience
▮ Professional dress
▮ Engaging colleagues and clients
▮ Displaying maturity
▮ Speaking articulately
▮ Showing a sense of confidence

Innovation distinguishes between a leader and a follower.

—*Steve Jobs, American entrepreneur, Apple co-founder*

My goal in writing this book is to include information from a variety of leaders and executives to give the reader real-world examples. There are some common threads among what these leaders from a wide range of industries want in their employees.

Jim Myers has been an executive and president of several Fortune 500 companies. He is currently President of Myers Management & Capital Group and leads several CEO forum groups comprised of leading executives who want to learn from him—and from each other. I asked Jim what characteristics he looks for in the people he hires and promotes. He remarked that this often-asked question took him to task with one of his executive teams. Here is his method, and a sound one at that.

It may sound simple, but it's not. When Jim and I spoke, he emphasized the biggest downfall for the people who do not display these traits is *consistency*. In other words, they may convey a positive attitude, a team player mentality, and dependability *some* of the time—but not *all* the time. The Reactor Factor requires that you understand your individual focus and match it with what the industry needs, what your shareholders want, and the company's goals. Myers says:

> *We began by building a list of the attributes of a stellar performer. We developed a long list of attributes, which I then suggested that we build into a hierarchy to determine the three most important traits. The top three attributes were: positive attitude, team player, and dependability.*

> 1. *Positive Attitude—This is not about being a "Pollyanna"; rather, it indicates people who come to work every day with the belief that they can do good stuff.*
> 2. *Team Players—These are people who love working with other people in a common purpose and genuinely delight when someone else on the team does something really good.*
> 3. *Dependability—These are people who always do what they say they are going to do.*

I have done this hundreds of times with different groups, and the hierarchy of the attributes always comes out the same. Next, we go to the other half of the board and list the traits of the people who don't make it. As you would expect, those attributes come out to be the opposite of the stellar performer.

1. *Negative attitude/cynical*
2. *Self-oriented versus other-oriented*
3. *Can't be counted on to do what they say they are going to do*
4. *Always miss the deadline*

Jim explains:

In hiring or promoting, I always assume that the resume is correct—I spend my time on the fit. I interview against the three top attributes of a "stellar performer" and [attempt to attain a] deep understanding [in terms of] what their behaviors have been on these traits. I can always teach people to do the work; but it's very hard to change their behaviors or beliefs. So seeing if they are going to fit is really critical. In fact, you almost never fire people because they can't do the work—usually you invite them into their future elsewhere because they don't fit and are generally dysfunctional.

I asked Jim about the parameters he considers with regard to layoffs. He referred me back to the list above, and informed me, "It is either all of the above, or the most recently hired. Layoffs should be done [with] some dignity to the event, and the provision—if possible—of economic comfort in the separation. [This way], former employees can seek other employment or some financial stability to help them in their transition."

LESSON

Be specific when you outline the criteria you expect people to bring to your team.

How does Myers' assessment of valuable attributes apply to you, and your situation? Ideally, you can respond in the following three ways:

1. Positive Attitude—If something negative happens, you ask for the information you need to make a decision instead of listening to the grapevine and naysayers. You communicate assertively to determine what your role is for the change. You don't become the cheerleader; but you do not buy into other people's fear and worry. Do you respond by focusing on the possibilities?

2. Team Player—I am always hesitant to speak about a "team," and prefer the phrase, "individuals working together." Human behavior dictates that we are more productive in a positive, productive environment than as a singular entity working alone. The problem comes when the team has to weed out the weakest links, or when the best players carry the ineffective people. So, what talents do *you* bring to the group of people you work with? Do you respond to the team's needs?

3. Role Model—Everyone watches your every move. We discussed this earlier, but I can't let an opportunity go by without discussing the importance of responding instead of reacting. Your actions become the character and ethical standards of the group, your colleagues, your subordinates, and when you are respected thoroughly, your superiors. The problem is that role-modeling behavior is not outwardly noticed, but the minute you falter, it certainly is.

Do You React or Respond?

Consider the differences between react and respond in Figure 4.1.

You can't control anything if you don't know first and foremost what your leaders want. If you are an employee, focus on your boss. If you are the boss, focus on the president of the company. If you are the president or CEO of the company, focus on your shareholders. If you are a teacher, focus on the administration. If you are a parent, focus on your children. If you are a teen or child, focus on your elders. If you are a student, focus on your faculty and parents. If you are a government worker, focus on the people you serve. Get the picture? I stated earlier that you can't control the uncontrollable. That is partly correct. Actually, you will have a better chance of managing the uncontrollable if you approach situations with a positive attitude, dig deep, and figure out how you can help.

- Every company is looking for hot talent. If it's not you, why not?
- Identify the talents needed to maximize your current position.
- Evaluate your own talents. Do they match the job you currently have?

React	Respond
Knee-jerk	Considered
Angry	Calm
Anxious	Eager
Quick fix	Considerations
I win	We collaborate
Stressed	Balanced
Retort	Report
Know-it-all	Asks thoughtful questions
Negative	Positive
Judgmental	Open-minded
Makes excuses	Takes personal responsibility
Jaundiced	Ask questions and clarify
Won't speak up	Shares appropriate information
Rude	Respectful
Immoral	Ethical
Clam up	Communicate
Fearful	Confident
Aggressive/passive	Assertive

Figure 4.1 Differences between React and Respond for Leaders

- If not, what will you do?
- Learn where your industry is going and continue to learn, learn, learn.

I interviewed Bo Calbert, President of McCarthy Building Companies Inc. Southwest, as well as a respected and successful leader in the construction industry. It was obvious from the interview that Calbert's caring attitude and internal drive continue to be a winning combination. He was quick to point out the skills needed in

industry today reach far beyond construction. I asked him the following questions about recruiting, hiring, and promoting employees:

When you hire, what are the key traits you seek in candidates?

- *We like our people to be well rounded, so we look for diversity on
their resume/past. [We're trying to find people with] leadership
skills, integrity, team mindedness.*
- *[We also seek a] strong aptitude for our business challenges.*

What are the attributes you look for in people you promote?

- *A passion for their work, [as well as] life away from work. High
integrity and people/leadership skills.*
- *Proven performance year over year. Having the ability to show
resilience during a setback by being able to bounce back and
move forward.*

What separates the people you keep from the people you let go?

- *For the people we keep—certainly past performance, their
proven commitment, and contribution and loyalty to the organization during tough assignments.*
- *The first level of people we lay off are those who have a consistent level of performance that is just not up to an acceptable
standard, and/or have consistently not reacted positively toward
taking action as outlined in their performance plan.*

LESSON

Remember the three Cs: commitment, contribution, and communications.

According to Arch Granda, President and CEO of Grandwest & Associates, "I place a great deal of importance on the ability to communicate effectively and act strategically; this is prevalent in my response to your questions." Granda has been a financial wizard and a turnaround expert for more than three decades and has held executive leadership posts at Westinghouse Financial and other Fortune 500 companies. He is known for his quick assessment and strategic agenda while quickly reading people and knowing who the best players are. I asked for his opinions on what leaders want.

What are the attributes you look for in people you promote?

▌ *Performance evaluations in existing position, including the ability to communicate and work effectively with new peer groups.*

▌ *A self-starter with excellent leadership and communication capabilities, including the ability to listen to his direct reports.*

▌ *The ability to think strategically with a good focus on the competition and competitive environment.*

▌ *One who can temper personal aggressive characteristics with an understanding that success often depends on getting things done by others—including direct reports and peer groups.*

When you hire, what are the three key traits you seek in candidates? (Answers assume that the new hire is not fresh from college.)

1. *Relevant experience and the ability to lead and grow with the company.*

2. *The ability to communicate effectively with colleagues and clients.*

3. *The ability to understand that the future success of the company has everything to do with strategically preempting competitors.*

Reducing staff numbers is always hard. What separates the people you keep from the people you let go? (Answers assume that this refers to salaried staff positions, and are tailored to this group.)

▌ *Substandard performers should always go first, irrespective of age, sex, tenure, and position. This should be an ongoing part of any organization—[regardless] of general staffing reduction programs. However, it becomes [even] more important during periods of general staff reductions; because you need to ensure that the remaining organization recognizes that under-performers have no future with the company.*

▌ *Ensure that staff [members who] are strategically important to the company are assured of their future. If retention bonuses are required (always a sign of executive miscommunication or a nonconvincing strategy), pay them to stay.*

▌ *If any position can't pass the test of importance (i.e., would the company be worse off without this position?), eliminate it and watch the good people you hired and promoted (using the above criteria) rise to the task.*

LESSON

Simplify, act, document.

Saul Blair, Executive Director of IPC The Hospitalist Company, is without a doubt a leader who takes learning and growth of himself and his staff seriously. He continues to be a student of leadership and personal responsibility. Saul's success is constantly tested, not by IPC The Hospitalist Company, but by himself. He has the fastest growing region and continues to cut costs and manage expenses.

When you hire, what are the key traits you seek in candidates?

- *Natural talent: absent of talent, even the best training will not raise performance.*
- *Work ethic: quality versus quantity. Individuals who like their days to be productive.*
- *Tolerance: candidate's pain threshold, how thick-skinned is the person. Every job contains multiple tasks; some are enjoyable, others far less so.*
- *Persuasion: advisers versus pleasers.*
- *Engagement: individuals who engage in their task and company.*

LESSON

Know what traits are important to the leader.

Renee Powers, Associate Broker, ABR, CRS, PC, Previews Property Specialist at Coldwell Banker Real Estate Group, continues to grow the business, and the economic downturns have much less of an effect on her business than most. I believe her perseverance, focus, and discipline are the winning combination. She had this to say:

I only hire if the person is a complement to my business. He or she must have the following strengths:

- *Self-motivated and a self-starter*
- *Doesn't need constant guidance or has to be micromanaged*
- *Sets check-in times so I can review his or her finished product*
- *Establishes mutual trust*
- *Willing to ask questions, no matter how insignificant*
- *Competent and capable of carrying out instructions*
- *Has a willingness to learn*
- *Enjoys working*

You will get a raise when:

- *You are doing more than is stated in your job description.*
- *You are exceeding expectations.*
- *You are solving problems to strengthen business and client relationships.*

LESSON

Know what you expect from employees, peers, and teammates. Don't waver from your focus and needs. It will help you keep the business healthy.

What Leaders Want

Judy Sitton, Honorary Doctorate of Humane Letters, Executive Vice President of SunGard Bi-Tech (retired), continues to show love for the people who worked for her. She remains close to the people she managed before she and her husband, Gary Sitton, sold the company. They host retirement parties and celebrate their successes. Judy's tenacity and spirit spill over to everyone she touches—even after her retirement.

While at Bi-Tech and SunGard Bi-Tech, I served as the Executive Vice President. I am reflecting on experiences that were particularly challenging and noteworthy before my retirement. Two areas that "bubble to the top" are the impact on the workplace and the spirit of the organization by those who are negative; and secondly, the absolute priority of exceptional customer service in securing a satisfied client base and employees.

On the topic of workplace negativity (on which you are an expert!), [a detrimental employee] can be the "cancer" in an organization. If there is any potential for a negative person [among your staff], you need to find a position for them wherein they can succeed but minimize their influence on others. More importantly, [you must] remove him/her from the employee mix whenever possible. "Making a case" involves appropriate documentation, follow-up, and setting realistic expectations that involve accountability and consequences. As one of Mr. Sitton's axioms states, "Encourage such a person to work for your competition."

Some of my more challenging responsibilities involved dealing with discontented and unhappy clients. I tried to be a good listener, generate solutions on issues of divisiveness, and recognize the importance of dealing with folks as I wish to be treated. If, for some reason, the chemistry of the relationship was unworkable, another manager would be asked to assist to move the project forward. The ability to be proactive in such situations and to provide options for solutions are helpful ways to provide support.

LESSON

An absolute priority should be exceptional customer service in securing a satisfied client base and energized employees.

Mike Campion, Founder and President of Killer Shade, is an unusual leader; if you don't believe me, just check out his web site at www.KillerShade.com. Success came early but it hasn't always been easy. He has done his share of knee jerking but has now figured out how to run a successful company. He is passionate about everyone understanding the core values and you will understand why after you digest them. Here are some comments from his web site:

Killer Shade Core Values—Saving the world one shade at a time.
   Who We Are—We design, manufacture, and install stupendously cool commercial shading products. We have entirely too much fun doing it, and we are quite possibly the most fun (and attractive) people you may deal with in a given day.

What We Believe:

Be Real: OK kids, here is a fan favorite. We Killers have all had jobs where we had to "fake it," act professional, and put on our "game face" every day we trudged into work. Our little Killer Kingdom was founded on being who we are. When we started January of 2005 we decided that we were going to quit trying to be professional, please everyone, and use excellent table manners. In our infinite wisdom, we came to the conclusion that by being who we are we would likely alienate 90 percent of potential customers—but the ones that "got us" would be loyal fans who would allow us to eke out a meager salary while doing what we love. Then the craziest thing happened. People actually liked it. They started coming in droves. Next thing you know—employees loved it, we started attracting the top talent. So what do you end up with—brutally honest people with high integrity that drop the mask. What you see is what you get. We understand we are not a fit for everyone, but we have made our peace, so if you are feelin' our vibe, browse on. If not, best of luck to you . . . try www.boringshade.com.

Be Passionate: This is huge!! We can't have people who aren't 100 percent. Go Killer or go home. This is all a part of our work hard play hard mentality. Nuff said . . .

Have Fun: This little gem ties right in with our marquee value of Be Real. We come to work and enjoy each other, and we do our best to enjoy the work we do and the people we do it with (that's you). We bring our kids with us on appointments. We taunt our customers on our web site (often in person). We drink beer after hours and play foosball during hours. We love what we do and love the community of employees, customers, and vendors that we do it with. If you are lucky, and we like ya, we might even invite you to join in.

Make Money: Money makes the world go round—certainly our Killer Kingdom. Without it, the magic is gone. If we aren't making great money, then we aren't bringing enough value or serving our customers the way they deserve!! We are committed to having the resources to be Killer in all that we do and money is a fabulous way to keep score. Our customers vote with their dollars. We get paid on results, not activity. If we don't have money, we aren't doing our job. It is as simple as that.

Help Out: This is key. Even though we Killers have way too much fun making way too much money while getting to be ourselves, *it's all for nothing if that is the end in and of itself. All these things are just plain silly if we can't contribute and give back. Helping out embodies the spirit of who we strive to be, with each other, our customers, families and people and organizations in need throughout our community. We are always looking for new and creative ways to help out and would love any suggestions from our loyal supporters ... uh, we're talking to you ...*

LESSON

Establish solid core values then eat, live, and breathe them.

Your Turn

Honestly answer the following nine statements about yourself:

1. I am proactive on accumulating and applying skills.
2. I am an excellent presenter with no fear of speaking in public.
3. I take the initiative and have no fear of sharing ideas.
4. I show confidence, not arrogance or timidness.
5. I am respectful, gracious, tactful, polite, and caring.
6. I learn names and remember personal references.
7. I am always on time, don't procrastinate, and never miss a deadline.
8. I ask for needed resources if I can't figure it out for myself.
9. I communicate according to the other person's style, not my own.

LESSON

As an employee, understand what your leader is looking for in all aspects of your position. As a leader, inform your people what you view as important.

Twenty years from now you will be more disappointed by the things that you didn't do than by the ones you did do. So throw off the bowlines. Sail away from the safe harbor. Catch the trade winds in your sails. Explore. Dream. Discover.

—Mark Twain, American poet

CHAPTER 5

The F Word

∎∎∎

The Skinny on Being Fat

Be not anxious for what you shall eat, or what you shall drink ... or what you shall wear ... Isn't life more than food? ... and the body more than clothing?

—Luke 12:22; 29

Fat—the ultimate F word. The Reactor Factor is all about turning negatives into positives. Did you react or respond in your mind when you saw "The F Word" as the title? Did you react or respond when you read the word "Fat?"

Here is the real deal. Did you know that some companies are penalizing people for being fat? Outrageous, you might say. The fact remains, however, that companies are taking this route in an effort to cut health-care costs and reduce the number of people having to be laid off. It is a bottom-line business decision. Does this resonate with you? Do these companies' choices to control the uncontrollable cost of health care raise your blood pressure?

Fat Chance for Reducing Costs

One in three people in America is considered obese. This number continues to soar, which, for employers, translates into health-care premiums growing twice as fast as inflation to nearly double their cost since the year 2000. An employers' goal is to hold down costs without offending or pushing away employees. In addition, if companies control costs, they won't have to lay off people.

Sixty-two percent of 135 executives responding to a PricewaterhouseCoopers survey in 2008 said unhealthy workers, such as those who smoke or are obese, should pay higher benefit costs, compared with 48 percent in 2005. So here is something you can control: lose weight if you need to, and stop smoking. "But Marsha, it's hard." Oh, I know. But again—this is something you can *control*.

Fact: At Indianapolis-based health-care system Clarian Health (www.clarian.org/), employees' pay is docked if they fail to meet certain weight-to-height ratios, and cholesterol and blood pressure levels, or if they smoke.

Fact: National insurer United Healthcare (www.uhc.com/) introduced a plan that, for a typical family, includes a $5,000 yearly deductible that can be reduced to $1,000 if an employee isn't obese and doesn't smoke. Bottom line: lose weight and stop smoking and save $4,000.

Fact: County workers in Benton County, Arkansas (www.city-data.com/county/Benton_County-AR.html) were offered a similar plan. The $2,500-a-year deductible can be reduced to $500 if a worker meets low height/weight ratios during yearly on-site physicals. Thomas Dunlap, Benton County's Human Resources Benefits Specialist, said the plan had witnessed a nearly 30 percent drop in claims, and led to marked changes in the workplace.

According to the 13th Annual National Business Group on Health/Watson Wyatt Employer Survey on Purchasing Value in Health Care, more than half of all employers use financial incentives to encourage employees to participate in one or more types of health improvement activities, and 24 percent more plan to do so in the coming years. Upon the writing of this book, there were over 16 million listings of diet and health blogs found on Google!

Additionally, the U.S. Department of Labor released final clarifications on the Health Insurance Portability and Accountability Act (HIPAA) of 1996. They ruled that employers can use financial incentives in wellness programs to motivate workers to get healthy. Some lawyers say, however, that weight-based compensation plans might run afoul of other employment laws such as the Americans with Disabilities Act (ADA).

Live by the following words of wisdom. I do:
Never eat anything you can't lift.

— *Miss Piggy*

A staggering $30 billion is being spent annually on weight-loss products and promotions; yet as a nation we are still *gaining* weight at a staggering rate. Childhood obesity has doubled in the last 20 years. There is little question that obesity is associated with a variety of negative health risks in both children and adults:

- Coronary heart disease
- Type 2 diabetes
- Cancers (endometrial, breast, and colon)
- Hypertension (high blood pressure)
- Dyslipidemia (for example, high total cholesterol or high levels of triglycerides)
- Stroke
- Liver and gallbladder disease
- Sleep apnea and respiratory problems
- Osteoarthritis (a degeneration of cartilage and its underlying bone within a joint)
- Gynecological problems (abnormal menses, infertility)

Health-care experts believe that it is premature to declare obesity a disease, and that doing so will only make the situation worse.

If you are trying to get fit, consider the TLC.

TAKE IT

You know you need to drop a few pounds, but right now you have so much on your mind that you choose not to deal with your overactive fork. You have a plan to tackle it in 30 days and mark it on your calendar. Your goal is to make an overall lifestyle change versus beginning another (unsuccessful) yo-yo diet.

LEAVE IT

You decide not to take any action at all, and to reject the idea of losing weight. After all, dieting is such a drag.

CHANGE IT

You pledge to yourself to make a lifestyle change. You make a flexible action list that will be your guide to feeling better and being healthier. You realize that it's not about dieting; it's about taking personal responsibility for your choices. *You* are in control of what goes in your mouth. Yes, you need to change some habits; and that is a good thing.

Some of your affirmations can include:

- I will save money, because eating more costs more.
- When I eat fast food, which will be less often, I will make better choices.
- I will feel better about myself, and know that I look better.
- My insurance premiums will be reduced, because I am not in a high-risk group.
- I will enjoy the children in my life and be a better role model for them.
- My productivity will improve because I will have more energy and be better able to focus. I know this can chip away at my earning potential and efficiency, so I choose to control it!

According to a Stanford University study, obese people with health coverage may already be punished on the job. Those surveyed were paid an average of $1.20 less per hour than nonobese workers. Why? Employers may intentionally adjust overweight employees' wages to account for health-care costs. Bottom line: it costs them more, so it will cost *you* more!

New health-care plans are different, because employers are demanding that workers participate in health exams—including having their weight checked and blood taken to screen for high cholesterol or blood sugar. Why not? Many companies insist on random drug testing already; how different is this? Would you change your eating habits if you knew there was random "weight testing"?

A Duke University Medical Center study found that obese workers filed *twice* the number of workers' compensation claims and had medical costs that were seven times higher than nonobese workers. "This link between obesity and workers' compensation costs means that maintaining a healthy weight is not only important for employees, but also for their employers," said Truls Ostbye, MD, Duke professor of community and family medicine and one of the study's authors.

Workers' compensation writers are addressing obesity and health issues in loss-review presentations with clients. "Obesity is a real risk management issue," said Woody Dwyer, senior ergonomics consultant with Travelers. Hospitals are becoming the focal points for obesity-related injuries, because medical workers must lift and move an increasing number of heavy patients. And according to the Atlanta-based Centers for Disease Control and Prevention, obesity kills approximately 112,000 people a year.

Many employers are taking proactive steps to address their workers' weight issues by trying to make it convenient to live healthier lives while on the job, according Mike Lemrick, Senior Vice President of Managed Care Services at Cambridge Integrated Services. "However, employers are more apt to focus on OSHA standards than on the issue of their employees' obesity," he explains. "We need to take the stigma of it not being politically correct and somehow address it matter-of-factly. For any employer, their employees are their most valuable resource."

Promotability

A survey of British personnel officers said they were less likely to hire and promote obese individuals even if they did a good job.

These startling findings were uncovered by *Personnel Today* magazine and The Obesity Awareness and Solutions Trust (TOAST), and reinforced what many knew all along: overweight people are discriminated against.

Sixty-five percent of adult women and 70 percent of adult men in the United Kingdom are overweight. That means that millions of workers are being held from promotion because of their body size! And how do our statistics in the United States compare? As mentioned earlier in the chapter, one in three people in the United States is considered obese, and this number continues to soar.

"With obesity directly affecting one in four women and one in five men in the United Kingdom, this is a grave injustice to millions of ordinary workers who could, at any time, find themselves unemployed and unemployable, or suffering from bullying at work. Besides that, it's just plain ignorant, hurtful and unjust. Obesity is hard enough to fight, without having to bear it as a social stigma," according to Anne Diamond of TOAST, who calls "fattism" the last remaining prejudice.

"I knew that fattism was the last remaining prejudice in this country. But I had no idea that it was legal—and openly practiced in the business world," she added. Here's the rub, though, for people like Anne Diamond. The last time I checked, I can't change my gender, my race, or my age. Even if I tried really hard, those three legislated prejudices can't be changed. (OK, maybe the gender issue, but I don't want to go there.) In most cases, the issue of corpulence, obesity, and fatness can be changed.

Of 3,000 human resource professionals surveyed, 93 percent said they would rather give the job to a thin person than a fat one—even if both had similar qualifications. Thirty percent said they would not hire obese individuals; and 37 percent said they were not sympathetic to overweight employees. Since there is no discrimination law for obesity in the United Kingdom, it is legal for employers to fire someone who is obese even without proving that the condition affects the person's work. Fair? Probably not. But this is the real world; it involves personal responsibility, self-awareness, and choices.

"The assumption is that someone slimmer will do a better job than someone fatter; and that simply isn't true. They're not even referring to obese people, but fat people; and with 65 percent of women and 70 percent of men in this country overweight, that's a significant proportion of the workforce being discriminated against. If people don't employ people who are overweight, they're not going to have a workforce," claims TOAST Chief Executive Louise Diss.

Another survey had 2,000 respondents answer questions concerning their personal experiences of "fattism," and how they felt that this particular form of discrimination had affected them.

- Two thirds of people concerned with their weight believe employers have a responsibility to help them stay in shape.
- More than half (55 percent) of people concerned with their weight believe fattism should be treated in the same way as sexism and racism.

- More than 60 percent of people concerned with their weight say they have been bullied, made fun of, or discriminated against because of their size.
- Nearly 80 percent of those taking part in the survey say weight is becoming more of an issue in today's society, and is 50 percent more of an issue in the workplace.
- Nearly one-quarter (23 percent) of respondents say their weight has held back or hindered their career opportunities.
- Over one-fifth (21 percent) claim that their weight leads to work colleagues and associates undervaluing their abilities.

Eighty percent of all respondents believe that a person's weight is becoming more of an issue in today's society, and 50 percent more of an issue in the workplace. As one respondent wrote, "Fat jokes are seen to be an acceptable form of humor, still with cover comments such as 'no offense' etc."

I do not personally believe that employers should be responsible for monitoring the health of their personnel. I do, however, feel that they can work toward reducing health-care costs by helping to pay for gym memberships, or even having the convenience of a gym on-site. When a company decides to help people in this matter, it is certainly in their best interest and becomes a real benefit to the entire company. In addition, when possible, it would be best to provide healthy food at break times or meetings. The traditional "donut and coffee" routine should be tossed aside with carbon paper and mimeograph machines. Companies *can* help employees make better choices.

Enough is known about healthy eating for companies to be able to provide a good variety of healthy choices in the workplace environment. Add that to the fact that large employers could work with sports and leisure facilities to organize low-price gym memberships in exchange for sponsorships—and that would be a real bonus.

Eliminate the thinking of the perfect body and the focus Hollywood plays on "thin is in." It is unrealistic and unhealthy. The same 30-second spot that displays a rail-thin, size 0 actress entices the viewer to the huge, oversized burger and fries. Talk about a mixed message. This is where our individual personal accountability and choices click in.

Here are a few more interesting stats (as if you haven't heard enough to get the message): A recent survey conducted by *Personnel Today* of more than 2,000 human resource (HR) professionals in the United Kingdom has revealed that "fattism" is manifested in the workplace. Of those interviewed, 12 percent believe that obese workers should not be in client-facing roles; 30 percent consider that obesity is a valid medical reason for not employing a person; and 11 percent think dismissal by reason of obesity is fair. Perhaps most alarmingly, a massive 93 percent of those interviewed—when faced with two identical candidates of different weights—would employ the "normal weight" person rather than the obese applicant. A staggering 47 percent of HR professionals interviewed as part of the *Personnel Today* survey believe that obesity has a negative effect on employee output.

I'm not going to address the possibility of discrimination under the Americans with Disability Act, because it is not clear whether obesity is a "disability" in terms of the definition under the act. However, here's a tip for employers: you should be aware that an obese employee who is treated less favorably than someone of normal weight *might* be able to utilize the law of equal pay or the law against sex discrimination. In the meantime, however, employers are advised to be aware of the legal implications of their actions, and to act positively to encourage a healthy and happy workforce.

LESSON

Fit people are warriors in life; they have mastered themselves.

Randi Smith-Todorowski is the owner of Atlas Martial Arts and understands the importance of health. She has always been healthy, but decided to become a weightlifter. Putting on 20 pounds of muscle made her feel a little too "manly." She stopped her strenuous weight-lifting routine and the extra weight became flab. Personal responsibility for her health quickly took grip. Her interview was crisp and to the point.

Smith-Todorowski's response to the F Word:

I recently heard there is no such thing as fat people, only lazy people. This resonated with me. When it comes to doing business and building relationships, I choose to spend my time with people that I have confidence in. It is challenging to respect someone who is grossly overweight and I'm OK with it. In my opinion, it is a total lack of personal pride. Fat indicates an 'I don't care attitude.' Fit screams personal pride, confidence, determination, hard work, perseverance, discipline, and self-respect. It doesn't take a genius to figure out how you approach life. After all, the way you move is the way you live.

As a third degree Black Belt in Kung Fu, I have chosen a life rooted in positive thinking and healthy living. The relationship I have with myself is extremely important, because it makes up 50 percent of all the relationships I have and will have with others. Although no one has the right to judge anyone based on appearances, we all have the right to choose our relationships based on performance and potential. The body is an outward manifestation of what is going on in the mind. An unhealthy body reflects an unhappy and unhealthy mind. More than just the physical health concerns that come from being obese, you also deal with depression and lack of productivity.

I love when people tell me that I am in such great shape, because I have great genetics. I smile and say thank you. I think of all the supposed overnight success stories; the same people thinking I have good genetics would assume that PT Barnum, Richard Branson, and Howard Shultz "got lucky." Do a little research and you will find that any great success story is backed by humility and hard work. The same is true for staying fit in a world of fast food and constant temptation.

I was reflecting the other day on the importance of discipline in terms of success. Be it sports, business, or health and wellness. To achieve desirable and significant results, you must make a commitment to personal goals and hold yourself accountable. Fit people are warriors in life; they have mastered themselves. Overweight people are victims of just the opposite. They have elected to self-sabotage. They make excuses, blame others, suffer from poor me syndrome, and have elongated pity parties.

Stop waiting and start taking personal responsibility. Take personal pride in yourself and your long-term health. Fall in love with you and the possibilities will be endless!

LESSON

There is a perception of people who are overweight, whether it is right or wrong. This is your life and you are on center stage.

Physical Activity for a Healthy Weight

What is your choice when it comes to health and fitness? Maybe you are already perfect and don't need any change. If so— congratulations. Your choices have been excellent; so keep up the great work!

> *The devil has put a penalty on all things we enjoy in life. Either we suffer in health or we suffer in soul or we get fat.*
>
> —*Albert Einstein*

The question remains: if you need to shed a few pounds, how are you going to respond to the situation? Are you going to change your lifestyle and not just "go on a diet?" Do you plan to stick to a sensible exercise plan, or to just react for a couple of days, kill yourself, then go right back to your comfort zone?

When you decide to turn something you can control, like your health, into a success factor, let me know. Choose to become your own personal trainer and cheerleader. You will be positioning yourself in a positive frame with your employer, your leader, and everyone you touch in your life. The message you decide to send is then one of, "I've decided to be healthy so I can bring the best me to the world, my job, my family, and my friends."

> *Today's beauty ideal, strictly enforced by the media, is a person with the same level of body fat as a paper clip.*
>
> —*Dave Barry, comedian*

CHAPTER 6

Office Politics and Gossip

■ ■ ■

The Silent Killers

The secret is out: Office Politics can kill your dreams and success. Gossip can ruin your high hopes. It often seems like an unnecessary evil; but in reality, you are the one who has to learn how to handle these career murderers. You must play office politics and learn to manage gossip to succeed.

> *It is just as cowardly to judge an absent person as it is wicked to strike a defenseless one. Only the ignorant and narrow-minded gossip, for they speak of persons instead of things.*
>
> —*Lawrence G. Lovasik, Slovak priest*

The Root of Office Gossip

When employees don't have the information to understand how a company is making decisions, moving forward, or generally operating, they will fill the gap with gossip that is spread through the grapevine. Add office politics to the mix—and an environment of backstabbing, negative undercurrent, low morale, lower productivity, and other detrimental effects ensues. However, there are specific steps for you to apply in order to stamp out these dreaded killers.

When I interviewed Mary Ellen Dalton, CEO of Health Services Advisory Group, one of the questions I asked was the way in which she manages the flow of information in her office. Her answer was one that all business people need to hear and apply: "We have established a culture of: If you don't know, or you need the information, ask. There will not be retribution of any kind." Because of the problems they've had in the past with employees filling the gaps with negative and incorrect information, Dalton said that this approach has eliminated office politics—and the negativity associated with it.

LESSON

What kind of culture are you creating? You are 100 percent responsible for how you handle workplace infections.

Office Politics

Office politics isn't about winning at all costs. It's about maintaining relationships and getting results at the same time.

According to *Wikipedia*, the phrase "Office Politics" is defined as "the use of one's individual or assigned power within an employing organization for the purpose of obtaining advantages beyond one's legitimate authority." My question is this: who determines "one's legitimate authority"? This sounds a little constrained and arbitrary to me.

And here is my favorite part from *Wikipedia* ... "Those advantages may include access to tangible assets, or intangible benefits such as status or *pseudo-authority* that influences the behavior of others." What? Where is the leader? Haven't the employees approached the office-politics bottom feeder to call him out on his behavior?

Here is a more helpful definition—as far as I'm concerned—from BNET Business Dictionary: Office Politics are "interpersonal dynamics within a workplace [that] involves the complex network of power and status that exists within any group of people." Ah ha! So it seems to stem from the people that drive office politics and they receive their instructions from leaders who construct the culture. (See Mary Ellen Dalton's comment.)

The person who says, "I'm not political" is in great danger. Only the fittest will survive, and the fittest will be the ones who understand their office's politics.

—*Jean Holland, independent human resources professional*

Office Politics and Gossip Quiz

You may not consider yourself to be a major player in office politics, but you might be surprised. Respond to the following nine comments:

1. I always keep my cool, and never take personal attacks to heart. __Yes __ No
2. I communicate effectively and am able to always respond appropriately to office politics and gossip, whether or not it is aimed at me. __Yes __ No
3. I stay calm and do not get angry when I hear others talking about people or maligning the company. __Yes __ No
4. No matter what others say or do, I remain courteous and civil. __Yes __ No
5. I can easily stay on issue, no matter how personal or unjust it may seem at the time. __Yes __ No
6. After a negative incident and ugly rumors are heard, I can stay realistic and upbeat. I shift my negative thinking to positive. __Yes __ No
7. I never gossip or pass on rumors at work or at home, and I establish a clear path away from the negative grapevine. __Yes __ No
8. I understand that office politics will always be present; I just choose not to be part of it. __Yes __ No
9. I understand that the grapevine and office politics can be a positive communication tool and know how to use it. __Yes __ No

If you said "yes" to the nine questions, then you can skip this chapter and move on. Even if you did say "yes" you may want to freshen up your toolbox with some new ideas. If you had even one "no"—keep reading this chapter. And I'm glad you're here!

How to Navigate Your Way Through Tricky Political Waters

So what can you do to manage this human ritual? Here are the techniques I've recognized for managing this career disease. We need to understand that this ritual of politicking is essential for everyone in business.

LESSON

You can turn a 23-foot speedboat on a dime but it takes a lot to get that cruise ship turned around!

KEEP YOUR COOL

Train yourself not to get sucked into the toxic situation and detrimental behavior. When you feel yourself succumbing to a "fight or flight" reaction, take a deep breath, count to 10, and say to yourself, "This is a test. This is only a test. This will not be important in 10 minutes, 10 days, or 10 years." When you buy into others' bad behavior and become a participant in the grapevine or gossiping, you give your power away. You become part of the problem.

Anger is a great force. If you control it, it can be transmuted into a power that can move the whole world.

—*William Shenstone, Scottish writer*

Train yourself to not take comments or criticism personally, because they really aren't about you; they are simply a reflection of someone trying to upset you for a particular reason. Take the old "water off a duck's back" approach. This evil toy or poor behavior used in the business is unsettling and will derail your self-confidence. Train yourself to plug into a mantra or a memorized phrase such as, "No matter what you say or do to me, I'm still a worthwhile person."

LISTEN

Tune into what the other person is actually saying. Stop all the internal chatter and mental terrorism, and don't just skim over their message. Don't become upset, because you will totally stop listening! Put your own opinions aside and hear the other person's side of the story, from his or her perspective. By doing so, you will learn from office politics and gossip rather than being upset by it. When you have mastered listening, then learn how to communicate effectively.

LEARN TO COMMUNICATE

Question the intent of the message by using techniques such as fogging, a skill that helps you diffuse the situation or the message— just as fog does the sun. Overlearn phrases like, "You may be right, help me understand . . ." Stick to your guns and keep digging to find out more. Information is power! If they say, "Oh just never mind. It's not important," then you are the one who must bring closure to the topic. Respond by saying, "It must be important, or you wouldn't have brought it up!" Then use the broken record technique by repeating the fogging language, "Help me understand . . ." Train yourself to ensure that a conclusion is reached, or I guarantee the subject will come up again and again. If you say nothing in response to comments like these, then you are essentially agreeing with the instigator. Don't become a zipper lip! (I discuss dealing with the toxic behavior of a zipper lip in my book *Toxic People: Decontaminate Difficult People at Work Without Using Weapons or Duct Tape.*)

Good communication is as stimulating as black coffee, and just as hard to sleep after.

—Anne Morrow Lindbergh, American writer and aviation pioneer

Rommie Flammer, President and Chief Operations Officer of China Mist Brands, cites that the biggest hurdle in their first ready-to-drink bottled tea, China Mist Pure, is communications. She said:

Communicating our vision, and why it was worth all the extra effort and cost to create a truly great product, was probably the biggest hurdle.

We have so much to be positive about at China Mist Brands! Unlike many of my business associates, I feel we are in a truly unique and fortunate position. Having just launched two new product lines we have a lot of new things to talk to our customers about and new channels of distribution opening up to us as well. The type of products we sell, specialty tea and coffee, continue to grow in popularity and people continue to switch from sodas to more healthy alternatives so our category is strong. We primarily sell to the foodservice industry, mostly mid-scale and up, and they have indeed been hit hard so same-store sales are down but we will more than make up for this with new methods of distribution and increased market share.

The folks at our company look forward to coming years with much excitement and our people feel good about our future. They can, however,

97

*get caught up in the media so communication at CMB is top priority!
I communicate regularly with the team and share everything, not only
our successes but our challenges as well. We have taken a look at our
business top to bottom, fine-tuning our spending and focusing on driving
efficiencies. In the event we are faced with some tight spots down the
road, we will be more prepared to weather them.*

LESSON

Fine-tune everything and use constant communication to keep your
group informed.

OFFICE POLITICS CAN DAMAGE YOUR CAREER—TRUST ME!

Earlier in my career, I worked as a sales trainer—a management
position at GTE Directories Company (GTEDC). During the attempt of the Teamsters Local No. 957, International Brotherhood
of Teamsters, Chauffeurs, Warehousemen, and Helpers (Union),
to organize our sales people, I had been instructed not to defend
GTEDC with regard to the company's position on the union vote
because of legal issues. One of the organizers caught me in the hall
and was explaining the sales department's need for the union. In
my opinion, his data was incorrect, and his perspective judgmental. I just listened, and tried to be considerate and gracious. The
union person interpreted my silence as agreement, and used the
grapevine to spread the word that I was a union sympathizer. When
my manager heard this, I almost lost my job. His expectation was
that I would at least refer the person to human resources. Lesson

learned—*always* make your position known, even when you are fairly sure that the other person knows what it is. You don't want to be unpleasantly surprised in the way that I was!

We have two ears and one mouth so that we can listen twice as much as we speak.

—*Epictetus, Greek philosopher*

PLAY NICE

There is always room for courtesy, graciousness, politeness, and common etiquette; remember that this is your responsibility. Your co-workers will mirror your behavior and do the same. Be persistent in this approach. Pay special attention to your tone of voice, body posture, and word choice. People are smart; they can see right through insincere behavior. I also believe that passing on gossip or negative comments about the company, your boss, or anything concerning your job is political suicide. Look at software Eudora Moodwatch, and the ranking of the chili peppers.

Here's how it works. Eudora will rate both incoming and outgoing messages. You will see an ice cube or chili peppers next to the "Send" button as you compose messages. The software will (usually) mark the questionable language, similar to the way the spell checker marks unrecognized words. As delivered, Eudora will warn you when you try to send a "hot" message, but it will not delay sending the message. This is a useful tool to let you know if your words in that e-mail are "spike" words and if you are not playing nice. Have you ever sent a letter or e-mail prematurely and were sorry later? This tool is excellent for checking the perception others may have of your word choice.

FOCUS ON THE ISSUE—NOT ON THE PERSON

Remove the emotion, and if the situation continues to escalcate, keep restating the problem at hand. Address behaviors and outcomes needed, and if it gets too heated, call a time out and schedule a time to resume the conversation. When you are addressing office politics, it is often easy to slip away from the focus of the problem and get into the "he said, she said" conundrum.

FORGIVE AND FORGET

If you've been maligned, it is up to you to address the issue at the source. Shake hands, and move on. Carrying grudges—or worse, returning fire—will only damage you and your reputation. If you are having a difficult time approaching the topic, try this: "I have a sensitive issue to bring up. Is this a good time to discuss it with you?" If they say yes, continue with, "My goal is to create a productive environment for myself and hopefully others. I've heard that ..." and launch into the issue *without* pointing fingers, or using statements like "you said."

NEVER GOSSIP

Although gossip and spilling the beans can be titillating, it can also be cruel. Think of office gossip as verbal spam or junk mail and hit the "delete" button. When gossipmongers realize that no one is listening, they'll quiet down and get back to work. Remember, if you don't want people to gossip about you, you must refrain from gossiping about them.

Marilyn Puder-York of *The Office Survival Guide: Surefire Techniques for Dealing with Challenging People and Situations* says, "If you have more than three people in the office, the politics emerge. Simply put, office politics is the game of the workplace—the people, the culture, and the rules that must be learned. That rear-kissing co-worker, the strict dress code, the secretary who supposedly just answers phones but really runs the office."

She offers five tips for surviving office politics:

1. Think before you act (or speak).
2. Nurture the stakeholders.
3. Keep enemies close.
4. Imitate the successful.
5. Play the game.

OFFICE POLITICS HAPPENS

Don't spend time worrying about office gossip. Obsess on this age-old killer and you never have time get your own work done. If the water-cooler conversations on what is happening in the company are distracting and time-consuming, pry yourself away and get back to work. You are not paid to discuss "what if" decisions made by shareholders, bosses, or managers. If you are concerned with what you hear, then ask a reliable source, and do it in a way that creates a cycle of communication. Stay open to what you hear, and continue to question.

The Ultimate Communication Tool

Yes, office politics is as simple as patting someone on the back when that person has done outstanding work and announcing publicly that they've done well. A study of human resource managers and professionals completed by Roffey Park, United Kingdom, found that less than a third of the group felt office politics could never be used constructively, while more than half—58 percent—had experienced this age-old gossip tool to have been useful and positive. Sixty-one percent of the 856 people polled admitted to having been involved in office politics, but claimed that it had led to a constructive outcome for their organization.

Here are nine simple rules of the office politics game:

1. Know your teammates.
2. Scout out the competition and know their strengths and weaknesses.
3. Help your teammates hit their goal.
4. Be prepared to play the game at meetings and be involved.
5. Fill in for them when they are out.
6. Take on unpopular plays (projects).
7. Don't drop the ball. This is a game breaker.
8. Take ownership and don't blame.
9. Shake hands when you lose.

Controlling and Pruning the Grapevine

You already know that gossip is idle talk, buzz, or chitchat—especially about the personal or private affairs of others. This chat forms one of the oldest and most common means of sharing—usually unproven—information, and it's known to introduce errors and inaccuracies in otherwise factual information. The term also insinuates that the news transmitted has a personal focus,

102

as opposed to normal conversation. The question is—how do you manage gossip?

My own business always bores me to death; I prefer other people's.

—*Oscar Wilde, Irish dramatist, novelist, and poet*

Gossiping in the workplace can prevent you from being considered for an otherwise deserved promotion; even worse, it can get you terminated from your job. Remember that the way you conduct yourself professionally is an important reflection of your work ethic.

Guide to Managing Gossip

▌ Excuse yourself when the conversation turns to gossip.
▌ Stick to the topic of business or current events.
▌ Stay away from discussing personal issues like finance or health.
▌ Call the behavior by asking the person gossiping to include the person being discussed.
▌ Express your loyalty to your employer.
▌ Try to keep your "work friends" separate from your "personal friends."
▌ Avoid being the target of gossip by being professional and friendly.
▌ Stay light and friendly, while sticking to business.

The best tactic to managing gossip with regard to your success is to avoid discussions with co-workers that might be construed as critical to others or that put down the company.

Kim Silva, Operations Team Leader of Fairytale Brownies, began her employment with Fairytale Brownies in February 1994, giving her resounding expertise in the manufacturing arena, but more importantly, leading people by applying communication excellence. She oversees daily operations for these yummy treats, including production (baking and shipping), customer service, human resources, and facility operations.

I was most interested in how she managed communications, because this skill helps control the grapevine and gossiping. The following information was provided by Silva when asked how she managed a negative, failing economic outlook:

> We began by making changes to some of our catalog offerings when we started to see the buying habits of our customers change. We tried to adapt as best we could and were actively advertising "Over 30 Items for Under $30." We also started running sales and promotions much earlier in the season than normal. With all the extra efforts on the sales front, we still saw a drop in sales and came in behind our projections.

Silva continues:

> Since the holidays have come and gone, we have been forced to implement further changes in order to survive. After conducting a small RIF (reduction in work force), we had a meeting with all remaining staff to explain the state of the company and get ideas for further cost cutting efforts.

The following is a list of what they have done:

- Reduced overall headcount by about 20 percent.
- Pay cut for all senior level managers and exempt staff, including the two owners of the company.
- Reduction in work hours for hourly team members.
- Renegotiated with current vendors for better pricing.

▪ Eliminated various services that can be completed in-house (e.g., cleaning services).
▪ Everyone will skip one anniversary bonus payout.
▪ Job sharing across departments.
▪ End of Month All-Staff lunch is now a "themed potluck" versus the company buying lunch.
▪ Use credit card points for employee perks, business travel, and various company purchases.

And here is the best part of what Silva shared:

I will stress that the most important thing we have done is be open and honest with our staff. We post daily numbers and keep them informed of the state of the company and how they can help. We believe that by being proactive, diligently watching our costs, and promoting new sales channels we can be our survival. The entrepreneurial spirit is alive and strong at Fairytale Brownies!!

LESSON

During good times and bad, communication maintains creativity, boosts morale, and creates a positive environment.

Creeping Gradualism:
The Disease Behind Gossip

Although you know how to best handle office gossip, you may still be wondering—how does this kind of chatter even begin? And why do we fall victim to participating in it so easily? Well, it all comes down to a lack of effort, really; when you get lazy, your skills—communication and otherwise—aren't used. You expect others to fill the communication gaps for you, and when it doesn't happen your internal voice gets upset. You *need* to know, so you listen to—and sometimes even create—"stories" to get the scoop you need. As you have guessed already, this can breed an environment of unrest that damages your self-confidence, worth, and esteem—often to the point of becoming a skeptic and taking the negative route that drills a bigger hole from which you must eventually excavate. And there we have the beginning of gossip that will contribute to the never-ending cycle of negative office politics.

Waste no more time arguing about what a good man should be. Be one.

—*Marcus Aurelius, Roman emperor*

You're likely thinking—me? *Lazy?* In fact, most people don't make a decision to take a job by saying, "Yeah, I'll take this job so I can be idle, uninformed, get involved in gossip, and ultimately get fired." Being lazy is not something people *choose* to do at first. There is a terrible disease called Creeping Gradualism, and the infection comes from relinquishing the chance to take control of every choice and action in life. It gets worse when you bury your head in the sand and resort to comments—either internal or external—like:

- "They didn't tell me."
- "How was I to know?"
- "I can only work with the information I have."
- "They didn't ask me."

106

Soon, accepting the status quo becomes easier than managing change, asking questions, or taking the initiative. An easy escape route is to snake around the grapevine, make up or embellish stories, and aggrandize the little information you have—which turns you into the gossip creator. Not a good place to be, but it has totally been your choice. The decision to react to a situation versus responding has just earned you the title of "gossipmonger." Is this *really* what you want?

Think of your job like a bank account; you withdraw from it what you've put in. My advice would be to deposit a lot of skills in the job bank account. Make yourself rich with your capability to handle yourself and others.

Nothing succeeds like the appearance of success.

—*Christopher Lasch, American social critic*

And what about your memory bank? Creeping Gradualism can make you *think* you have all the skills needed for success. Not so! When you share negative—or positive—traits about other people, your listener attributes those same traits to you. Here's how workplace gossip backfires, and how office politics is exacerbated.

The American Psychological Association published a study about the "boomerang effect of gossip." It turns out that when you say something—for instance, "He's a selfish, mean jerk" or "Her husband is cheating on her because she's an icicle in bed"—your listener often attributes those qualities to *you*. Are you ready for that to happen? Researchers call this "spontaneous trait transference." When you're indulging in workplace gossip, your words could be interpreted as a description of your own personality and actions. Is that what you want?

You know that words can devastate, upset, infuriate, or annoy people; but what do they do to you? There are three types of stress-inducing words that can break your spirit, sabotage your goals, and damage your health. This is true even if you're working at home, so don't go to the watercooler! Be aware of these words and eliminate them from your thinking and your communication:

- Rude—when you don't think before you speak and say something inappropriate about someone else.
- Complain—when you are whining about anything. Remember that most people don't care.
- Judgmental—watch your words and ask yourself whether you want the same kind of information said about you.

The only time people dislike gossip is when you gossip about them.

—*Will Rogers, American entertainer*

Gossip doesn't just spread negativity and put you in a bad light; those damaging statements actually impair your physical well-being. "Maintaining a negative mood for a long time is harmful to your health," says Psychology Professor Scott Hemenover of Kansas State University. "The key isn't how stressed you are, but how long you are stressed. Staying stressed for a long time can impair your immune and cardiovascular functions." The level of cortisol—a dreaded stress hormone—can compromise your health and make you sick.

So, how do you rank on the gossipmonger scale? Are you doing yourself and your colleagues more harm—emotional *and* physical—than good?

Are you a Cortisol Creator?

I do not spread malicious gossip. __Yes __ No

I do not make "harmless" slips of information about others. __Yes __ No

I do not snub people who may be not to my liking. __Yes __ No

I always give appropriate credit to colleagues and subordinates. __Yes __ No

I do not pass on negative information of a personal nature. __Yes __ No

Cortisol floods your system when you're merely *thinking* about a negative or stressful event. When you imagine throttling your colleague or secretary perhaps (because they're spreading gossip!), your body can respond physically with conditions like hypertension, depression, insomnia, fatigue, and gastrointestinal disorders. Your words cause similar reactions. Mockery, cynicism, thoughtless comments, or disrespectful words all cause feelings of internal pandemonium, which negatively affects your health.

In fact, I recommend learning as much about the effects of gossip as you can—because it may just save your life.

No one gossips about other people's secret virtues.

—*Bertrand Russell, English logician*

Your Turn

Answer the following if you would like practice in applying the ideas discussed in this chapter and earlier in the book. This is the only way to learn to respond positively to the negative situations you may encounter at work. Check Free Stuff at www.MarshaPetrieSue.com for some suggested answers.

I can no longer deal with a fellow employee who talks behind my back.

_____

_____

I don't get along with my manager.

_____

_____

My manager doesn't like me.

_____

_____

My work environment has turned hostile and I have to tell someone what is going on.

_____

_____

Live that you wouldn't be ashamed to sell the family parrot to the town gossip.

—_Will Rogers, Cherokee-American cowboy, humorist, and social commentator_

CHAPTER 7

Is Your Networking Working?

▪ ▪ ▪

The Good, the Bad, and the Connected

Being totally overwhelmed with the plethora of choices in networking today seems to be the norm. There are hundreds of online social networks to which you can connect. Then, layer on the networking meetings along with the up-close-and-personal time with people; and you can be in the down draft of the networking typhoon. Consider the possibilities:

▪ Chamber of Commerce
▪ Small Business Administration

▮ Convention and Visitors Bureau
▮ Business Journal
▮ National Association of Women Business Owners
▮ Rotary Club
▮ Elks Lodge
▮ Lions Club
▮ Association Clubs/Association Meetings
▮ Religious Groups

Are you confused? Which ones are best for you?

Personally, I have wasted so much time in meetings that I felt obligated to attend for whatever reason. It finally dawned on me that I would be best served by homing in on the gatherings that not only I *like*, but that seemed to be the best match for my business and personal needs.

I met Debby Raposa, MAS, President of Idea Source, Inc., networking. I asked her if she would share an idea on how she and her company are responding to the economy. She replied, "The best way I have responded to the market is to attend functions where I am more visible to the community. It is a natural and easy way to connect with people—especially when you become involved with committees or leadership positions in associations or non-profits. It is a holistic approach to life—a win/win for all parties involved. Business then comes naturally."

LESSON

Network with a purpose to create visibility for you and your company.

112

Is Your Networking Working?

I believe that establishing a baseline of who, what, when, and how you build your network will help you save time and turn otherwise negative events into positive opportunities. You already know that many of the networking events in which you currently partake are a total waste of time, while others may help you achieve your professional and networking goals more quickly.

The following is not a quiz so much as an outline that is meant to help you dig deeply into your own thinking to determine where you want to spend your time connecting. This is solely for you, so mark all that apply, but please be selective. You might be tempted to circle them all—and this will not help you narrow your focus.

The reason(s) that networking is important to me is to:

A. Uncover job opportunities within my company or business.
B. Uncover job opportunities externally.
C. Sell my product or service.
D. Research my industry to gain intelligence about competitors.
E. Learn more about other industries and job possibilities.
F. Build my current business by growing the database.
G. Connect with like-minded people.
H. Other.

In building my network, it is important for me to include:

A. People for whom I have done favors.
B. People who have done favors for me.
C. Businesspeople I admire.
D. People who can hire me.
E. Vendors I may use in the future.

F. People who I want to know about my products and services.

G. Insiders who can refer me to qualified people.

My considerations prior to attending or joining a networking event:

A. I know that learning as much as I can prior to spending my time networking will help me in the long run.

B. My goal is to attend as many events as I can, and then determine what works.

C. When using online social networks, I have/will sign up for everything I can find, and then determine what works.

D. I need to understand the "personality" of the meeting so I can dress properly.

E. I will be ready to introduce myself in a creative, brief fashion.

F. I have questions prepared so I am ready to be a good conversationalist.

When I think about the time I spend networking:

A. I know it's time to leave when I have made a planned number of connections.

B. I will stay as long as the event has people.

C. If I have not met the kind of people I'm targeting within a specific time period, I will leave.

After the networking event, I:

A. Follow up with e-mail to everyone I've met.

B. Follow up with the people I want in my network.

C. Automatically add people to my database.

D. Do nothing yet, because I need to determine the best plan.

E. Have a shoebox full of business cards that need to be organized.

Try to put well in practice what you already know. In so doing, you will, in good time, discover the hidden things you now inquire about.

—*Remy de Gourmont, French novelist*

Your Turn

Planning is the key to maximize your time networking. Spending some time prior to beginning this important step to maximize your business success is essential. You can download these forms from the web site www.MarshaPetrieSue.com; and click on Tools for Success.

The reasons that networking is important to me:

∎ In building my network:

_____

_____

∎ My considerations prior to networking:

_____

_____

∎ When I think about the time I spend networking:

_____

_____

■ After the networking event. This is critical and must be well thought out if your goal is to maximize your time networking. I:

_____

_____

Communicate Clearly When You Attend an Event

No matter how you answered the previous questions, there are several important points to keep in mind when going to a networking event—and vital steps to take afterward. Whether you're attending for the first time or are a seasoned "networker," it's essential to remember the following:

■ Be personable, but not personal. That is—keep the conversation about professional topics, and remain friendly without delving into others' private matters.
■ Notice the person's tone, posture, hand movements, eye contact, and so on, and mirror them (without mimicking).
■ Avoid hasty opinions and judgments, but do rely on your first impression and gut instinct about another person.
■ Ask questions and focus on gaining, not giving, information.
■ Give well-placed, genuine compliments whenever possible.
■ Develop a clear 20- to 30-second sentence or two about yourself.
■ If you're on the phone, take notes. If in person, get their card, and when finished, privately make notes on the card. Reason? In some cultures, such as Japanese, writing on a business card is considered defacing the individual.

Follow Up

What are your next steps? Do you have a plan for all those business cards? Networking without follow up is a waste of your precious time. So unless you can answer the following, I would recommend cancelling your attendance at that next networking event.

▮ Deliver what you promised, if appropriate.
▮ Send personal handwritten notes and include a coupon or discount for your business service.
▮ When appropriate, ask for referrals and receive permission to use their name.

I never perfected an invention that I did not think about in terms of the service it might give others . . . I find out what the world needs, then I proceed to invent.

—*Thomas Edison*

Volunteer

Another way to network and interact with people from different business communities is by volunteering. In this pseudo-professional environment you can demonstrate a certain level of the skill sets you possess as a professional. The upshot is the people you meet might be from entirely different industries you haven't brushed shoulders with before.

▮ Be on the advisor board of the networking group.
▮ Write articles or press releases.

117

❚ Comment on the blogs of people you meet.
❚ Mentor or provide business coaching.
❚ Design your elevator speech (more on this later!).

Hi! My Name Is Marsha. What Do You Do?

Your mini-intro—also known as an "elevator speech"—is a well-prepared series of phrases about yourself and your company that becomes a natural part of your conversation. This is the perfect cure to help you network more effectively and to make your message memorable. In my research, I find that most people know how important it is; they just don't do it!

So—Are you prepared? For the unprepared, this awkward moment can be a lost opportunity to gain new customers, grow your business, or learn something that can benefit your success. Brief encounters can have the potential to become big wins. Your polished approach can either get noticed and increase your profits—or not.

People say conversation is a lost art; how often I have wished it were.

—*Edward R. Murrow, commentator*

PRACTICE MAKES PITHY

To prepare this powerful verbal tool, write down a list of everything you would like someone to know about you and your business. Keep it simple and concise. Then write the benefit for the person you are speaking to, not just the features. Remember the old acronym: WIIFM—What's In It For Me! You must tune in to their frequency to have them hear what's unique about you. Everyone has his or her own radio station and if you want your message heard, bring the broadcast back to the listener. Where is the value for them? Making their life easier, more balanced, more in control, giving them the tools to succeed, be happier, or whatever—you turn what you do into a benefit for them!

Decide what you want to say and practice it out loud, using a conversational tone. Even better, record yourself—then you can hear exactly how you sound to others! It is important to verbalize these thoughts; just thinking them is not enough. And it doesn't matter where you practice—only that you do. When your mouth speaks the words, you get powerful results. You begin to say and hear these positive reflections about yourself and your business—and you begin to believe them. Remember, what the mind perceives, the mind believes. Your confidence grows, and your business will, too.

PLANNING YOUR MINI-INTRO

A mini-intro or elevator speech is an interest-creating remark and includes an overview of an idea for a product, service, or project. This quick introduction can be delivered in the time span of an elevator ride. For example, thirty seconds and 100–150 words is a typical mini-intro. Overlearn these few sentences into a polished beginning to you and your message.

▮ What do you want people to know about you and your business?

_____

_____

▌ What benefit does this provide them?

_____

_____

▌ What is the next step you want/need them to take?

_____

_____

MARSHA'S EXAMPLE

The following is an example of how I use this process. As my business and services change, I re-craft my message. In addition, I have several different messages depending on the situation.

▌ *What do you want people to know about you and your business?*
That I am an author and professional speaker, and am available for them to hire me for keynotes, concurrent sessions, training; that I help people individually in communications, including presentation skills; and that my resources, books, and so on, are available on my web site and in bookstores.

▌ *What benefit does this provide them?*
Success, personal development, self-awareness, better relationships, improved communications, reduced conflict, personal responsibility, and maximized success, leaving entitlement behind.

▌ *What are the next steps you want/need them to take?*
Consider me for their next event, meeting, retreat, conference, or convention. Also, refer me to the right people, or consider hiring me themselves if they are the planner.

CRAFTING YOUR MINI-INTRO (ELEVATOR SPEECH)

The time to begin this process is now. Just begin anywhere. Many times the last part you want to write is your hook, so pick up your pen and start writing.

▎ Attention-grabbing question, quote, or data point:

_____

_____

▎ My name is _____

▎ I work with _____
　– That want to _____
　– By providing _____

▎ Is that something you (your company, team, etc.) needs to achieve?

Marsha's example

My name is Marsha Petrie Sue and I'm known as the Decontaminator of Toxic People.

I work with companies and people . . .
　Who want to build relationships in the workplace, reduce conflict, and drive successful outcomes
　By providing resources, including keynotes, individual coaching, books, CDs, and DVDs to help them succeed.

Is that something you (your company, team, etc.) need to achieve?

Then—stop and listen. *Don't* continue to provide more information about yourself, but rather ask questions about them. Your entire answer to "What do you do?" should take less than 30 seconds. So get to work, and craft yours. Train yourself not to drone on and on, sharing details about your business that no one will listen to—and that no one really cares about!

Social media offers new opportunities to activate . . . brand enthusiasm.

—*Stacy DeBroff, founder and CEO of Mom Central*

Social Networking: The New Way to Connect

In researching for this book and my presentations, I sent out a question asking, "What Social Networks on the Internet do you use to stay connected?" A quick response came back from my clients and contacts, who said this: "That's easy. I e-mail my friends, clients, vendors, and all the people in my business world." However, they don't realize that their comment is just the tip of the iceberg!

Jeff Hurt, Director of Education and Events at National Association of Dental Plans, is often asked, "What is Twitter, and why are you wasting your time with it?" His response:

The answer that I provide is usually followed by, "I don't get it."

Twitter, like any networking tool, is what you make of it. It is not just a broadcast channel or promotional tool. Rather, it is a conversational community, a free social networking service, and micro-blogging site arena that allows users to send updates—or "tweets," as they're called on the site—in 140 characters or less to each other. They transmit these messages in a variety of ways, including SMS, instant messaging, e-mail, the Twitter web site, or any one of the multitude of Twitter applications now available. Many people use Twitter on their mobile devices, as well as on the Web.

The Twitter gurus—or Twitterati, as they are often called—use Twitter for a number of reasons, including listening and learning, humanizing their brand, engagement, crowd sourcing, customer care, and as a way of keeping customers informed. I started using Twitter to learn more about my profession, industry, and social media tools. The beauty of Twitter is that by using "Twitter search" (search.twitter.com) you can find other people (known as "Tweeps" or "Tweeple") by sending tweets on the topics that interest you. You can follow those people, click on their links in their tweets (URLs embedded within the tweet and shrunk by a variety of applications), and then engage in a dialogue with them.

LESSON

Learn about social networking yourself, or, better yet, hire someone who can help you take advantage of everything available.

The value of a social network is defined not only by who's on it, but by who's excluded.

—Paul Saffo, quoted in The Economist

The reasons and benefits to become involved in social networks are:

■ They allow you to easily connect to existing friends and family. This becomes more difficult as life becomes more hectic, so apply these new tools, and start today.

▮ They help you keep in touch with other people through the use of publicized updates on your personal life and private-message exchanges.

▮ They are a valuable tool for building professional relationships. Finding other professionals to complement your abilities has never been easier, as many social networking web sites allow for searching by trade and skill set.

▮ They are useful in locating business resources. Business profiles have become popular in social networking web sites, so finding a business firm to suit your needs by location or specialty is just one benefit of such services.

▮ They provide opportunities for marketing cheaply and effectively. Most social networks provide the opportunity to include your business name, details, and contact information. By creating a business profile, individuals and businesses alike will have yet another way of finding you—typically for free.

Through social networking, sites allow you to tap into network systems of online friends, colleagues, clients, and group memberships to stay connected. I firmly believe that "touching" your clients on a regular basis helps build a more solid relationship. Some networking can also help you find a job, or even establish business contacts.

Our success has really been based on partnerships from the very beginning.

—Bill Gates, co-founder of Microsoft

Look for any additional features that these networks may offer. The most popular extras include music and video sections. I don't use the music capability myself, but I do take advantage of the video section quite often. (Is your head reeling yet?)

The entire social networking process has moved far beyond the stereotype of a teenager who is merely looking to expand his or her network of online "buddies." People of all ages and backgrounds have discovered that they can enrich their lives through the contacts they make on a social networking web site. Here are some ideas of what is available, at this exact moment in time!

> *The important thing is not being afraid to take a chance. Remember, the greatest failure is to not try. Once you find something you love to do, be the best at doing it.*
>
> *—Debbi Fields, founder of Mrs. Fields Cookies*

FACEBOOK

This site currently boasts around 250 million members. It was initially intended for college students; then it branched out, and now allows anyone membership. Facebook includes a custom API (application programming interface) that allows third-party developers to create unique applications for use within the site—a feature that differentiates Facebook from any other social network service online today.

MYSPACE

This site is massive—over 200 million members—boasting the largest membership of any social networking site on the Internet. MySpace has become well traversed by "Netizens" of all ages, genders, and other demographics. In addition to keeping in touch with existing friends and relatives, the social networking web site has also become a means for making new connections, both personal and professional. Due to its enormous user base and overall high visitor count, MySpace has become a major target for spammers trying to reach a large audience.

MySpace is the Wal-Mart of social networking sites.

—*Chris from www.MoreRon.com*

TWITTER

A free social networking service that allows users to send "updates" (text-based posts that are up to 140 characters long) via SMS (small message service) instant messaging, e-mail, the Twitter web site, or an application such as Twitterrific. The site has become popular in only a few months—a lot of people are watching it with 7 million unique visitors monthly.

Twitter for Business Success

Recipe for successful Twitter application:

1 Filipino marrying into a Korean family

1 taco truck Goliath Cater Craft

1 scoop Korean Taco

1 tortilla

1 RockSugar chef Roy Choi

A dash of friends and family to blog, brand, and Twitter.

Mix in the Internet social networks and you have a delicious application of using social networks to establish and run a successful business. Where will this unique taco truck park next? Only the tech-savvy know for sure.

In other words: A notably successful Twitter campaign started when, after a night of bar hopping, founder Mark Manguera was sitting with his 25-year-old sister-in-law, Alice Shin. His wife Caroline was already sleeping soundly. Mark was munching on a Carne Asada taco, and it dawned on him. Why not put Korean barbecue on a taco? He told friends and family of his epiphany, and put the magical recipe together.

The result: the Kogi Korean BBQ taco truck (@kogibbq on Twitter). After celebrating a November 20, 2008, soft opening, the roving cater craft has emerged as a social-networking juggernaut, drawing 300 to 800 people each time it parks. This may occur several times in an evening and launches a mushrooming cyber-hippie movement affectionately referred to as "Kogi kulture."

LINKEDIN

With 28 million members, this site is a powerful tool for business networking—and it's also one of my personal favorites. LinkedIn is an online network of professionals from 150 industries around the world. Ranked as the 164th most visited web site worldwide, the service simplifies the process of maintaining existing connections, while making it easy to form new relationships. Reconnecting with professionals is as simple as typing in their e-mail addresses or other personal information to look them up. As an early adaptor to LinkedIn, I initially had no clue what it could do for me; I have since found it to be incredibly useful.

FRIENDSTER

This group has about 75 million members, and was considered the top online social networking service until around April 2004, when it was overtaken by MySpace. Demographic studies indicate that users are from 17 to 30 years old. Despite the fierce competition, Friendster's primary focus is helping people to connect with friends, family, classmates, and people sharing similar interests.

It's wonderful to meet so many friends that I didn't use to like.

—*Casey Stengel, baseball player and manager*

hi5.com

At 50 million members, this site operates as an international social network with a local flavor. It enables members to stay connected, share their lives, and learn what's happening around them. It allows members to find friends and content by providing "a platform for established artists, underground talent, and everyday people to all gain prominence amongst a worldwide audience." Data Junkie, a blogger with a personal soapbox, said that hi5 has dominance in more countries than any other major social networking service— including Columbia, Ecuador, Portugal, and 12 others.

Stumbleupon.com

With 2.75 million users, this web browser plug-in allows users to discover and rate web pages, photos, videos, and news articles. It's a great way to get web site promotion, and was bought by eBay for $75 million in May 2007. Unbelievable!

> *For everything you have missed, you have gained something else, and for everything you gain, you lose something else.*
>
> —*Ralph Waldo Emerson, American poet*

digg.com

Digg has about 36 million unique visitors and was made for people to discover and share content from anywhere on the Internet by submitting links and stories and voting and commenting on submitted links and stories in a social and democratic spirit.

Ecademy.com

This is a professional social network with 500,000 monthly users. More than 60 percent of the members are in the United Kingdom, with the United States representing the second largest user base at nearly 10 percent of total users. Ecademy includes both a free basic membership and a paid premier membership. According to *Information World Review,* the premier membership is required for access to create clubs or to view personal business introductions and private meetings.

Classmates.com

This site has about 40 million members and is one of the oldest social networking sites around. Classmates.com was kicked off in

1995 and has proven to be a great way for members to connect with old friends and acquaintances from throughout their lives. My high school reunion was organized through Classmates.com, and they made it very easy—and fun—to see all who were going to attend. The best part was getting to look at the "old" pictures!

Ning.com

With one million networks, this is an online service that allows you to create, customize, and share a social network—about any topic that you like. For example, Phil Singleton of John Driscoll and Company started a group using Ning.com that he called the Arizona Excellence Group. Singleton hand selects whom he wants to invite, and within six months of its inception, he had 60-plus people in the group. Luckily for me, I was invited to become a member. We are a tight knit group and continue to refer each other for business opportunities, support, and problem solving—and also work with one another. This is an excellent example of using social networking for business development. What group could *you* form with Ning.com?

LESSON

What social networking group could you form? Create your own fan club. Be original and imaginative.

---

del.icio.us.com

At 1 million users, the web site del.icio.us (pronounced as "delicious") is a social book-marking web service for storing, sharing, and discovering web bookmarks. It was founded by Joshua Schachter in late 2003 and is now part of Yahoo.

Meetup.com

This site has 2 million members, with **943,233 visits per day**, and is an online social networking portal that facilitates offline group meetings in various localities around the world. Meetup allows members to find and join groups unified by a common interest—such as politics, books, games, movies, health, pets, careers, or hobbies.

Two more tips to keep in mind when using social networking sites:

1. Have your own, private e-mail account that you use for these. I recommend not using the company e-mail unless you are the owner of the business. Either get a Google (Gmail), Yahoo, or Hotmail account free of charge; or purchase a domain that can be yours forever. Then, use that email for secondary contact with any business contacts you might want to retain across time. Do your work on your work e-mail, but keep a "stay in touch" channel alive.
2. Sign up for business networks and blogs—and join mine. You'll find me on Linkedin.com, facebook.com, plaxo.com, twitter.com, and youtube.com. Not to mention, a site I hope you're already familiar with, www.MarshaPetrieSue. com.

I asked Susan Caldwell, Publisher and Founder of *Applaud Women*, "What Social Networking groups are you using and what are they doing for you?" She shared the following information:

> *I'm currently using LinkedIn, Facebook and Twitter. I'm also on MySpace, but I don't really use it much. I like Facebook the best; I find it's easier there to communicate with everyone at once. I was [also] able to create a page for an Applaud Magazine Group. Though I like asking questions through LinkedIn and have received good information from it [I found it to be somewhat] time-consuming. And for those of you who are not on Facebook, because you think it's just [for] college kids—that is no longer true. Many businesses are now using it on a daily basis; it's free and easy to set up. I am open to all—just search my name and e-mail (sjcald@comcast.net) and go to groups, Applaud Magazine, and join my group.*

Personally, I think it will take a couple of years for people to figure out the business applications of these sites. In projecting how this normally works, industries will start to segment using the vehicle and social media used most frequently by their "people."

LESSON

Change your habits of sending your messages by using new methods and social networks.

Many people unfortunately (and erroneously!) consider all types of networking—whether in person or on the Internet—to be a pain. When you attempt to discuss it with them, they react negatively. Although this is totally their choice, my position is that you should learn as much as you possibly can, don't let your past negative experiences get in the way, and just go for it. What do you think? Tweet me @mpsue and let me know.

And don't expect anyone to tell you what you need to do—you are the one who holds the key to responding to this seemingly overwhelming task!

Stay tuned!

CHAPTER 8

What You Need to Succeed

▪▪▪

Presentation Skills, Meetings, Managing Negativity, Dress Code, and Customer Service

What are the skills you have that will allow you to move from a negative position or point of view to a positive one? Have you even thought about it? I guarantee that your leaders and bosses consider everything you do, how well you perform, and every skill you possess. Have you considered how you will fare when it's time to trim the forces and free up people's futures?

LESSON

You are entitled to opportunity.

Steven Gitt, MD, FACS, of North Valley Plastic Surgery and Surgery Center is a star in the field of plastic and reconstructive surgery and works to create a culture of accountability, success, and joy in his practice. Dr. Gitt began our interview with the preceding quote—one that completes and encapsulates what you need to succeed. He has helped his staff with a shift in mindset by giving each employee total accountability for running his or her area of the workplace. Gitt said there is often an attitude of "I am, therefore I get" in the medical office environment (and, I believe, in many businesses today)—so he challenged each of his employees to pinpoint exactly where they could save money in their department. He said that everyone dug deep and really made an effort on this proposal. They are now saving the practice between 15 percent and 40 percent, which amounts to about $20,000 or more per month. Gitt did mention that a few people quit, but he ended up with employees who truly supported his efforts. As a leader, Gitt identified what was needed to succeed.

LESSON

Determine what you can do to succeed.
How do you become a star?

Your skill set and attitude will determine if you survive. This is the simple truth—so put your pride aside; leave your ego at the door; and get ready to polish your skills so they are bright and shiny. Providing you with real-time information from high-profile leaders has been an ongoing theme, so here comes the real deal! Whether you work for a small or large company, are an entrepreneur, experienced, or just starting your career, this information is vital for your success. Test yourself for each point made, and if you are not 100 percent comfortable with your skills and profile, change it.

Ten-point skills assessment (consider how you really are, not how you should be):

1. My verbal communication is polished, and I consistently achieve the outcomes I need. __Yes __ No
2. I am confident in presenting to anyone, any group, at any time, and any place. __Yes __ No
3. If there is conflict, I always have the skills to resolve it quickly. __Yes __ No
4. I know which approaches work best when I work with difficult bosses or colleagues. __Yes __ No
5. When team members are not performing to benefit the team, I have ideas that help them as individuals and the overall group. __Yes __ No
6. I have excellent skills to manage meetings, even when I am not in charge. __Yes __ No
7. I am always looking for ways to cut expenses and drive profits for my company. __Yes __ No
8. I dress appropriately, even on casual days. __Yes __ No
9. I have a personal library and continue to invest in my learning. __Yes __ No
10. No matter what my job title is, I know I am in customer service. __Yes __ No

How did you do? What can you improve upon to help yourself be more successful? Your future lies *totally* in your own hands. Don't wait for someone else to tell you what you need. Figure it out yourself; pay attention to what today's business leaders say; and promise yourself that you will change what is necessary. After all—it is *your* life.

Platform Presence: Your Presentation Skills

How comfortable are you speaking in a public venue? How about if you are asked to present your views on a project you may be working on? What if your professional association asked you to keynote a meeting or present a concurrent session? Merely upon hearing these suggestions, most people become sick to their stomach, feel their knees to begin to shake, and their mental terrorism starts screaming, "No way!"

Here is the quickest way to separate yourself from other people in the workplace: hone your public speaking skills, and become comfortable with presenting. I've learned that it is simply another skill to tuck away in your toolbox.

Question: You are the leader of a team project and eight people. Your boss told you that one of the team members must be laid off. You have an important client presentation just around the corner, and you need the entire team to present a portion on the project. There is one member who is completely paralyzed when they get in front of any size group. Otherwise, the entire group is fairly equal. Who would you suggest that the boss let go? This is a no brainer! Of course, it would be the person with the presentation skills that are not up to snuff.

What You Need to Succeed

How are your presentation skills? Answer honestly! Can you:

- Quickly format a three-minute presentation while sitting at a conference table with your boss or client? __Yes __ No
- Begin with a dynamic "hook" to get the audience's attention? __Yes __ No
- Leave the group with the action you want them to do? __Yes __ No
- Channel your nervousness into energy from the platform? __Yes __ No
- Remain calm if there is a troublemaker in the audience? __Yes __ No
- Connect with the audience using appropriate humor? __Yes __ No
- Show the authentic you from the podium? __Yes __ No

I can guarantee that if you learn how to present using authenticity, humor, and great information, then you will be ahead of everyone in your arena. Learning this skill early in my career paid off. It helps you remain visible to the people who make the decisions in the organization, not only in terms of promoting you, but also in tough times—when deciding who gets laid off and who doesn't.

As a Certified Speaking Professional, I have learned what it takes to be memorable. Here are six considerations for creating a stellar presentation:

1. Before you speak, consider the following:
   a. Whenever possible, learn the attitudes, needs, and beliefs of the audience, and identify their issues. Focus on what *they* want versus what *you* want to deliver.

    b. Understand the layout of the room in advance when you can. This small task will help you feel more confident during your presentation. Practice in this environment if possible.

    c. Rehearse your presentation—even if you are not sure if you will speak—whether it will be extemporaneous or planned. Lack of preparation is the number one reason why speeches go bad—and why people are overly nervous.

2. Anxiety: Learn how to control yours; this is a learned skill, to be sure. Understand that the audience can tell immediately when you are highly nervous. This unrest is typically caused by lack of self-confidence, which is then exacerbated by poorly drafted presentations, little or no practice, and not knowing your audience. Think about a nervous speaker you previewed; did their anxiety build confidence in their message?

3. Construction: Use the following 11-point model to plan your presentation. You will see later in this chapter that it can also be used for planning meetings.

    #1—Closing. It may sound strange, but you actually want to *start* your planning by determining how you'll end your speech—in other words, what you want the audience to remember. By doing so, you will save time putting your presentation together.

    #2, #3, #4—Key Points. Establish the three key elements of your presentation so that it becomes memorable for the listener. Remember that people generally remember things in groups of threes (see information under meetings).

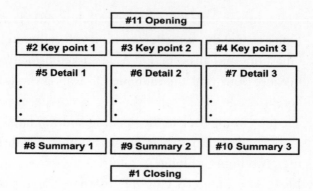

Figure 8.1 Presentation Model

#5, #6, #7—Details. These sections include your data, examples, and information pertinent to the three issues identified above.

#8, #9, #10—Summary. Develop this part by thinking about the three issues; and, in one sentence, ask—what do you want people to take away from each?

#11—Opening. What is your hook and the sound bite that will move the audience to the edge of their seats?

The presentation model is outlined in Figure 8.1.

4. Delivery is the key. The flow will keep audiences engaged and interested in your message.

a. The hook (opening) is how you draw in your audience. Without a hook, you remain in the league of the norm and forgettable. A hook delivered with graciousness and a pleasant look leaves the audience spellbound.

b. The key points help the group know what the structure of your presentation is and keeps them interested.

141

   c. The summary tells the group what they need to remember. Don't expect the audience to think of this themselves.

   d. Questions and answers (Q&A) are asked *before* you close because you want the audience to walk away with your core message.

   e. Tie the closing back to the opening and you have a memorable and exciting presentation, whether it is three minutes, two hours, or longer!

   f. Flow: Use Figure 8.2 to give listeners the capability to stay with you and follow your material. This also gives you confidence in your material.

     (1) The opening is your hook. You take a deep breath and feel comfortable.

     (2) Tell the audience the three key points you will cover— it's like their mental agenda.

     (3) Now relate the details for each of the three key points, including the data, examples, humor, and stories.

     (4) Review a brief summary for each of the key points.

     (5) Ask for Q&A, and comments.

     (6) Close with what you want them to think, feel, or do.

   The presentation model is diagrammed in Figure 8.2.

5. The number one success element to help perfect your platform skills is authenticity! Be yourself. I recommend that you watch people who are compelling, or listen to their speech on an audio file. Dissect what they are doing and learn, learn, learn.

6. Pledge to yourself to be a lifelong learner. This ongoing learning gives you information to think and speak on your feet.

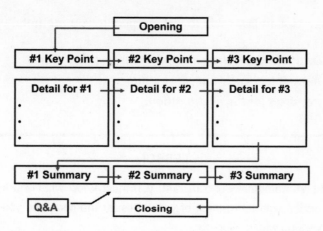

Figure 8.2   Diagram of Presentation Model

Betty Chan-Bauza, Vice President of Strategy and Product, Life-Lock, knows what she is talking about. She has worked internationally in a variety of industries, so pay attention to her ideas! During our interview, I asked her what she looks for in the people she hires. Chan-Bauza quickly sounded off with these three key attributes:

1. *They have to be smart.*
2. *They have to take initiative.*
3. *They have to be willing to roll up their sleeves and get it done.*

I then asked her for a profile of the people she considers "Stars."

▌ *Confident but humble.*
▌ *Think before they speak and know their audience prior to communicating.*
▌ *They have to have a trend of accomplishment.*

I asked Chan-Bauza, "How about people you promote?"

▮ *Loyalty through their actions versus just their words.*
▮ *They act tactically but think strategically.*
▮ *They dress for the next position.*

LESSON

In today's competitive job market, you must know what you know and understand the benefit of your skills for the company you are interviewing with or work for.

Be deliberate and premeditated in your mental processing.

Dress appropriately (and you thought dress was no longer important!).

Death by Meeting: Learn How to Run and Attend Meetings

A major business publication estimates that more than 11 million meetings are held in the United States every business day. We all attend meetings that are boring and a waste of time. Reviewing the painful aspect of poorly planned meetings solves nothing. Understanding what makes successful meetings is time well spent.

Cost of meetings:

▮ Add together the per-hour salaries or hourly pay of all the people who attended a meeting.
▮ Multiply the figure by two to account for benefits and general overhead paid by the company.

▌Multiply this figure by the number of hours the group met.
  – Example: $50,000 (avg. annual salary = $24/hr) × 6 attendees × 2 (benefits and overhead).
  – Think of a meeting you attended where little was accomplished.
  – Compute an estimated cost of the meeting. $_____.
  – Was this money well spent?
  – How could this money have been spent more wisely? What proactive steps can you take? Compute the estimated cost of a two-hour meeting ($576).

You can be a star quickly by showing your colleagues and leaders how much money is being wasted in meetings. Here are 12 time- and money-saving tips on how to plan an effective meeting.

1. Always outline the meeting objective.
   a. Things get done and time is saved because people know what to expect.
   b. Participants feel energized and valued because there is focus.
   c. Attendees will contribute freely, find solutions, and make decisions.
   d. Give people the right to challenge their attendance at a meeting, especially if it does not sync with their job, projects, or directions.
   e. If you are not in charge of the meeting (this is what Stars do):
      (1) Review the agenda. If there is nothing that is pertinent to your job and projects, question your attendance as the best use of your time.

(2) Be prepared to ask questions. Link them back to objectives, mission, vision, or other important company directives. Or better yet, include your knowledge from another project that can be applied to this one.

(3) Volunteer when appropriate and don't just sit there like a lump. Show your initiative. Don't wait to get recognized.

2. When people are determined to bring their hidden agendas, you must be firm in sticking to the meeting agenda. Establish a "parking lot" so their issues are written down and can possibly be discussed during the meeting, at a later meeting, or off-line and out of meeting time.

3. Control time-wasters, know-it-alls, and bores with ground rules (see #7).

4. Preassign a point person to bring latecomers up-to-date when they finally arrive. This helps prevent wasting other people's time. Or better yet, set a fine for late arrivals. (When I worked for Westinghouse Financial Project in Atlanta, the fine was $100—the money was given to charities!)

5. If you are not in charge of the meeting:

   a. If no one else is calling attention to the above ideas, take the initiative and bring it up.

   b. If you are saying to yourself, "I'll be fired"—hear me saying to you, "No you won't. It's what people do who take personal responsibility for their time and success."

6. Distribute the agenda 24 hours before the meeting. This allows the thinkers and process-oriented people time to assimilate the agenda and consider their questions. This does not mean they can add to or change the agenda. If

additional ideas are requested, they go on the agenda for the next meeting.

A committee of three often gets more done if two don't show up.

—*Herbert V. Prochnow*

7. Set ground rules.
   a. Ask the group if they would like to spend less time in meetings. (If you don't get a response, quit. These people are too inept to work with.)
   b. On a flip chart, ask them about the rules they would like to establish to run the meeting. These rules should be set by the attendees and revised for each meeting. If anyone veers off track, anyone can ask the group if they still choose to adhere to the ground rules.
      Meeting ground rules:
      (1) Stick to the agenda.
      (2) Begin and end on time.
      (3) Do not repeat an issue already reviewed.
      (4) Provide concise answers (no rambling).
      (5) Let each attendee finish their thought.
      (6) Do not interrupt.
      (7) What is said here stays here.
      (8) Keep an open mind. Don't judge.
8. Ask for Q&A before the meeting closes with action items. You want people to walk away with what they need to do instead of the answer to the last question.
   a. Give participants note pads to record their questions.

b. Create a parking lot to be used for items that arise that are not on the agenda. These items will be put on another meeting agenda.

9. Set time limits.

a. Limit comments to two sentences.

b. Appoint a timer so no comment runs over a predetermined amount of time. Suggestion: Hold each comment to less than two minutes.

c. Stick to the ground rule to begin and end on time!

10. Consider disrupting the meeting configuration and arrangement.

a. Have a stand-up meeting (they take less time).

b. Change the venue (park, restaurant, different conference room).

c. Vary the facilitator (draw numbers so everyone has to lead a meeting).

d. Do the same with meeting minutes, planning, follow-up, and so on.

e. Critical! Ask yourself if the meeting could be an e-mail instead.

The least productive people are usually the ones who are most in favor of holding meetings.

—*Thomas Sowell, American economist*

11. Meeting minutes.

a. Record the meeting and send a downloadable file.

b. Have each section of the meeting documented by a different person.

    c. Video tape the meeting (if you try this, people will be constrained at first).

12. Meeting planning.

        Start planning your meeting agenda by determining what you want the group to do, think, or understand. Ask yourself, "What do I want them to walk away with? What action do I want them to take?" This is the same format discussed above in presentation skills. Use the same template to plan your meeting.

Then think about what needs to be covered to reach this objective. When possible, work on keeping the focus in three key areas. For example:

■ Past, present, future
■ Products, sales, goals
■ Hardware, software, application
■ Manufacturing, sales, customer service
■ Planning, strategy, tactics
■ . . . you get the idea

The reason to focus on just three areas is that people generally remember information in groups of threes. Think about how literary folks have done with such stories as "The Three Little Pigs," "Three Coins in a Fountain," "Goldilocks and the Three Bears," and so on.

When It's Positive to Be Negative

In my book, *The CEO of YOU: Leading Yourself to Success*, much is written about the importance of a positive attitude. I never thought about a positive attitude ever being negative. Rick Labrum, Vice President Wealth Management, SmithBarney, gives you an excellent view, and as an expert in financial management, building wealth, and leveraging money, he is a true authority!

This interview with Rick Labrum made me think differently about how being positive may be a reaction (knee jerk) versus a response (learned). His unique perspective forces you to be realistic. Remember that a realist doesn't believe that the glass is half full or half empty. They believe you have the wrong size glass.

Rick began the interview by saying:

> *After experiencing several economic downturns over 40 years of business, one imagines they would be good at detecting leading indicators of serious economic change, which I believe is true. Reacting or responding positively once the indicators become apparent can be our Achilles heels. We act and think positively but the immediate perception of our action can be quite different. Being positive is a noble thought, however, positive actions that are very negative for many may be the result of our positive response to a negative situation.*

At this point he really had me curious and I asked him to continue:

> *Looking for and selling the "silver lining," finding something positive in a stressful environment and presenting it, with conviction, to our followers/clients/employees can many times cause us to respond in a manner that is not necessarily in our best (financial) interest. The "positive" attitude can cause us NOT to act or be reluctant to act because the action can create very negative results for many. Therefore, our response has become emotional and not rational. Positive can be negative. Of course, our escape is it could be worse, we could be laying off 1,000 people instead of 500 or even worse, I could be getting laid off. Ouch!*

LESSON

Challenge your own thinking. If you don't, someone else will!

Difficult Behavior: Are You a Role Model on How to Handle Toxic People?

The term "Toxic People" conjures up visions of emotional vampires and mental terrorism. You can't lead yourself to success if you let these people get your goat because buying into their negative behavior only makes you emotionally bankrupt. And getting ticked off feeds these difficult people's power over you.

The worst thing you can do when dealing with a toxic person is to become defensive or angry. This behavior only gives them power. If you start feeling upset, excuse yourself for a moment, count to 10, and return when you are feeling objective again. Train yourself to say to the mental vampire, "I'm not ready to address this right now. Let's meet this afternoon (or choose an appropriate time) to resolve this situation." And whatever you do, don't take it personally!

Think of mental terrorism as those little voices that are saying that you can't handle a situation or a person. This kind of thinking is often a sign of low self-confidence.

I like to visualize a big "T" that represents Triumph, not Terrorism. Choose Triumph and you will have the strength to manage your behavior and provide new communication parameters for them. Have you ever been a bystander during a conflict and you watch two people defend their positions, use poor communication

151

with voices raised, and then both walk away mad? What were you thinking about both of the angry colleagues' verbal skills? Were you thinking that the behavior was something you want to model? Probably not. So how do people perceive you when confronted with a difficult person or situation? Do they see you as someone who is in control and as someone they can count on to diffuse even ugly situations?

When you feel you *can* handle life's challenges, you create a mental environment that breeds success. This attitude builds self-esteem, self-confidence, and self-worth. The external application of self-esteem spills over into self-confidence.

Survival List—the Needed Nine

1. Maintain a strong belief in your own competencies and stop the thoughts of vulnerability and negativity. Take personal responsibility in taking control of the situation.
2. Review your talents and build from them. Check your strengths and use them in an upsetting situation. Know what you do well and leverage these strengths.
3. Cancel your membership in the whine and cheese club. "Oh, cheese, they're so mean." (You can hear the tone can't you?) Don't become a needy weenie and a victim of circumstance.
4. Keep your focus on being problem-oriented rather than danger-oriented. Understand that there is a problem to be solved, not a threat to your life or well being.
5. Rise above it. Pretend you are in a hot air balloon and lift your thoughts over the issue to get a new view.
6. Your attitude is totally your choice, under every circumstance. Be a winner not a whiner.

7. Hone your listening skills. If you aren't listening, you're missing out. Before you respond to a statement, ask another question: Can you tell me more about it?
8. Find the common ground. When you acknowledge commonality, you instantly diffuse the situation.
9. Give objective feedback. People will be more inclined to come to you with problems if they feel that they are appreciated and taken seriously.

There are two primary choices in life: to accept conditions as they exist, or accept the responsibility for changing them.

—*Denis Waitley, author and speaker*

Developing relationships with everyone is what successful people do. Are you ready to mend the bad ones and change your attitude about difficult people? I felt it was important for you to see that everything discussed in this book transcends all forms of business. Stephanie Studds brings to the U.S. Census Bureau an entrepreneurial spirit. Yes, it's true. The government is not always the bedrock of entitlement and there are people like Studds who produce a new enlightenment to the group.

Stephanie Studds, Chief of the Mailout & Data Capture Branch of the U.S. Census Bureau said:

When we hire and/or promote within our group, probably the most important factor is attitude and the ability to learn. Attitude covers a number of skills including communication, conflict resolution, customer service, and discipline. Quite often, it is easier to teach and provide staff with specific job-related knowledge and skills than it is to teach someone

153

the appropriate attitude that is required for success. A quality team player is paramount to the success of the organization. This begins with attitude. Someone who will go the extra mile for the organization acts on the team's behalf and not on their own volition. They strive to ensure that all members are well informed by communicating vital information to all involved. [I commented to her that this does not sound like a government agency!]

These staff members will also go out of their way to keep supervisors abreast of all developments pertaining to the team's work. A team member with the appropriate attitude will interact with others to protect the integrity of the team's reputation. Good customer service and conflict resolution skills begin with a good healthy attitude. Providing quality service in a courteous and understanding manner will often endear your customers to you and cultivate an environment conducive to accomplishing shared goals. Further, work ethic and attitude go hand-in-hand. Those with a team-centric focus will work tirelessly to ensure the advancement of all of the group's goals. These staff members are true assets whose work ethic and abilities tend to become models for the rest of the team and contribute greatly to advancement of the organization.

Wow, is that refreshing or what?

LESSON

It's all about tuning up your attitude and tuning in your communications. Dump the entitlement attitude.

Optimists are right. So are pessimists. It's up to you to choose which you will be.

—*Harvey Mackay, author and business owner*

154

Dreading the Dress Code

Negative: Defining the corporate dress code when it isn't clearly stated in an operations manual and procedures is tough. This gray area for leaders or employees is confusing because interpretation is left to each individual. The result is low morale, consternation, and a confusing environment.

Positive: The problem can be solved easily when personal responsibility is on the agenda. Consider the following six tips:

1. Take the lead and pay attention to how the customers dress.
2. Encourage a group of colleagues to meet and decide what the customers' expectations are concerning dress.
3. As a follow up, this group should develop a dress code suggestion list.
4. Pay attention to how your boss dresses and follow their lead.
5. Take the groups or your suggestions back to the powers that be and include a list of consequences determined by the team if the code is violated.
6. Hold a do's and don'ts fashion show and have fun with it!

The dilemma of business casual is a question that is frequently asked. Be careful not to go too far and dress too casually. Use the same set of actions as used to develop the dress code for establishing parameters for business casual dress.

Customers Count

Without clients and customers, nobody gets paid. With the exception of a small portion of industry today, you all have customers. The study done by the Department of Customer Affairs tells us that one angry customer can influence 67 other people. This is scary stuff. This study was done before the Internet was being used to spread "bad vibes" about companies and people. Did you know that an entrepreneur has licensed what he terms "suck" URLs for many of the top companies and leaders? How would you like a web site devoted totally to all the awful events you or your company does? Here are 10 simple keys to great customer service.

1. Answer the phone in 3 rings or less.

   AT&T did a study on this and found that by the fourth ring, people's blood pressure actually rises when the phone goes unanswered. Can you imagine? You haven't even had a chance, and the person is even more upset than they were at three rings!

   When the customer comes first, the customer will last.

   —*Robert Half International, Professional Staffing and Consulting*

2. Put a smile in your voice and on your face.

   Can you tell when a person is smiling on the phone? Do they sound like they want to help you, or that you are disturbing them? Put a mirror by your phone—yes, a mirror. Check yourself out before you pick up the phone. Make sure that your smile is heard loud and clear by the customer on the other end of the line. Remember what Eleanor Roosevelt said, "We teach people how to treat us."

3. Consider everyone as your customer.

   Vendors, the person sitting next to you, your boss, and your partner are all your customers. Not just the person you provide services and products to. If you treat everyone with respect and always find new ways to help them, you will receive the same back. You will develop consistency in your behavior, whether at home or at work.

   > *It is not the employer who pays the wages. Employers only handle the money. It is the customer who pays the wages.*
   >
   > —*Henry Ford, American industrialist*

4. Stay upbeat.

   Lemon eaters. Do you know these people? Sour faces. They always look angry. Do you like doing business with people like this? A positive nature and outlook gives you a leg up. And studies show that people who stay "energetic" lead happier more fulfilling lives. Life is too short to be a lemon eater!

5. Do what you say and say what you do.

   Do it immediately, do more than asked, and update the customer. If there is a delay in solving a problem, let them know immediately of the delay. Nothing is more frustrating than to have someone promise to "get back with you" and they don't!

6. Let employees handle problems on the spot.

   Nordstrom Department Store is known for empowering their people to make decisions on the spot. You hire great people so let them give clients choices to solve problems. I cringe when I hear, "It's not my job" or "It's against our policy." Do you think the customer cares? Absolutely not—they just want their problem solved, NOW! If you are not the boss, ask for this kind of latitude. Do research, like with Nordstrom, and give examples of companies that give employees to make decisions on the spot. Oh I know—it takes work! Your validated responses will help the company grow and make you a star.

7. Use the Fogging Technique to calm irate customers.

Angry customer? Use these words. "You may be right." An angry customer will hear they are right. That is not what you are saying. You are saying that there may be one tiny thin thread of truth, and you just need to know more. Then probe. Let them vent and when they have completed unloading their story on you, ask them this question: "Is there anything else?" Get to the real core of the problem so you solve the right problem!

8. Know what your competition is doing.

Visit their web site, ask for their brochures, call with questions, call the Better Business Bureau, and find out everything you can. You will find a chink in their armor and this will be your next product or service. You might as well do this because they are doing it to you!

9. Do the unexpected.

Call back days, or months, after a problem is resolved to see if there are any issues still bothering the customers. Take the opportunity to "touch" the client and leave a pleasant memory of doing business with you.

A business exists to create a customer.

— *Peter F. Drucker, American educator and writer*

10. The customer is always #1.

Return your calls, answer your e-mail, pay attention to the customer before you do anything else! I do considerable business with Federal Express, so naturally I visited their location in Chico, California, when I needed to ship a box home. I entered a shop that was totally under construction. The woman behind the counter was on a personal cell phone call, finished the call while we waited, and then told us they don't supply boxes any longer. We high tailed it out of that location, and went to UPS. UPS's employee not only said they had boxes, but also would wrap and secure the box for us. He filled out the form for us, and made the entire transaction painless. One situation can change a customer's loyalty in only minutes.

Consider improving client care by breaking the process into manageable steps. The following drill should be used with people and teams that work directly with clients so they can analyze and determine new methods to improve outcomes.

a. Write down a situation you had with a client or customer (remember this is anyone you touch) that did not have the outcome you desired. Think about whether you reacted or responded.

_____

_____

_____

_____

b. What were the implications for you and how can you change it for next time?

_____

_____

_____

_____

c. What were the implications for the customer and what can you do now, or what could you have done to create a better outcome?

_____

_____

_____

_____

Hawgwash was founded by Holly and Steve, whom I met when speaking at a Harley Davidson dealer meeting. Holly holds a master's degree in finance and has a proven track record in the corporate world while assigned as a controller in the telecommunications field. Her partner, Steve, is a retired Marine Master Sergeant who served a tour of combat in Vietnam and prior to retirement was assigned to the Pentagon. Together they bring a wealth of knowledge for those desiring to meet the challenges of the 21st century.

I asked Steve to what he attributed his success and he said:

You see, I spent years establishing "relationships" with my customers. I knew their cars and trucks but more importantly I knew them. I knew what they liked and disliked in service and I took care of them. By doing that, the dollars automatically followed.

Then I asked Steve how his business started and he replied:

The day I got laid off from the repair shop, I took my personal files with me and called each of my customers and thanked them for their loyalty and apologized because I would no longer be servicing their vehicles. Nearly 100 percent of them asked where I was going to be working, so a thought struck me. I called a friend of mine across the street and asked if he had room for a few cars. My friend said absolutely. I told all my customers that my new location was directly across the street from where I used to work. My customers followed me and the shop that fired me was out of business within 90 days. You see, I was more interested in providing a SERVICE and my customers were willing to pay for it. It's all about building relationships.

Since then, I have moved on to form my own company with Holly and we continue to this very day building relationships and providing service.

LESSON

The key to a good business is in developing personal relationships. Do not prejudge anyone and treat everyone fairly.

Homework for What You Need to Succeed

Choose the first skill you want to change. Make a list of actions you need to change and polish your skill and don't forget a deadline. When starting this process, allow yourself flexibility in changing the actions and revising the deadline. If you do need to make changes, stop yourself and ask "Why?" Your goal is to take any skill that if improved will help you take a negative situation and move it to be more positive.

Here's a homework assignment:

▌ The skill I need to change to succeed is:

_____

_____

_____

_____

▌ I need to improve this skill because it will help me:

_____

_____

_____

_____

▌ The actions I need to take include:

_____

_____

_____

_____

▌ My deadline for polishing this skill is:

_____

_____

_____

_____

I would recommend rereading this chapter and focusing on one element of success that, if you polished it, you could be just a little more successful. It's what you need to succeed. After all, you're in charge!

CHAPTER 9

Find It, Keep It, Love It

■ ■ ■

And What to Do If You're Laid Off

The world runs on individuals pursuing their individual interests.

—Milton Friedman, American economist, statistician, and intellectual

The employment landscape is competitive anytime but especially in a turbulent economy, so you must do everything you can to find a great job, perform to the best of your ability to keep it, and ultimately enjoy and love it. Any one of these three can throw you into a stalemate of career development, life balance, and success.

In addition, oftentimes as a leader at work or in your family, people rely on your expertise and guidance, so open up your perspective and thinking on how to apply these ideas to yourself or with others.

Bruce Crile, Vice President of Human Resources for the Doctor's Company, has been in business and human resources for almost 45 years. I was pleased when he agreed to provide his input and views on hiring and keeping employees.

Crile began by saying:

> I approach the executive promotion issue differently based on the position. Some assignments require a great affinity for personal interaction, others are more directive, and obviously there are degrees in between. However, the basics are standard, though they may be defined differently by individuals making the decision.
>
> In almost all cases, in the 45 years I have been in the business environment (44 years as a manager of some type), the standard trope "the past is a good predictor of the future," has proven to be a sound decision-making tool.
>
> > Qualified
> > Capable
> > Motivated
> > Trustworthy
>
> When I find a successful manager whose staff believes that he/she is at least as interested in their success as he/she is in his/her own, I believe I'm looking at a good candidate for more responsibility. When your staff won't let you fail you are almost guaranteed success.

Crile continued:

> The reverse of this statement is not always true but frequently is. There are successful people who drive their staff to his/her success, but in the

long run they have greater potential for problems. On the whole I'd rather take my chances on a "leader" than a "driver."

I also find I frequently get greater insight from people who work "for" or "alongside" the individual in question, than I do from their superior or written reviews (which incidentally I think are just a tiny bit better than worthless—for a whole lot of reasons).

Three Key Traits I Look for in Hiring

With his exceptional background and experience, Crile shared the traits he looks for when hiring:

I expect the potential employee to be able to jump the low hurdles such as: appearance, job history, qualifications, interview, background, and reference check. Beyond that I try to get a feeling for what drives the individual. It's hard to do, but I'm impressed if I get the sense that the person I am interviewing needs just couple of things from me: clear goals/instructions and room to succeed. In other words; understanding the destination and having me get out of the way.

I have one other thing I try to make a decision on; will I enjoy working next to this person for an extended period—which is more or less a gut reaction (using your friend Barbara Booher's term).

During a layoff what separates the people I keep from those I let go? Subject to applicable state and federal guidelines, the short answer is 'I try to keep those who provide the most value to the company.' This is usually a judgment call, and I try to include consideration of current value and future potential.

Wanting a different perspective from an entrepreneur and business owner, I interviewed Bud Rasner, DDS, owner of Knolls Dental Group.

What three traits do you look for in candidates?

Since I am in a health profession (Dentist), I am fortunate to be hiring licensed—and therefore fully certified—individuals; which generally means that they have the necessary training to go along with their license title. The primary attribute that I look for is the willingness to be a team member and get along with other employees. I am not looking for someone to come in and tell us how to run our business. When someone respectful and well groomed comes into an interview (in addition to having the appropriate skills by licensure training), they command my immediate attention. In direct order of key traits, I look for:

- *Nice, polite, and gracious*
- *Well spoken and the ability to communicate*
- *Cleanliness and hygiene*

What are the attributes you look for in people you promote?

I want employees who are able to interact peacefully with work-mates, follow directions, and complete assignments in a reasonable time. I welcome free thinkers that organize, but I like them to run it by me before they change existing systems unilaterally. I look at two primary things—quantity of work, and quality of work—along with evidence that they are not "toxic" as you would call them. They must exhibit the capacity to accept responsibility, and know that account-ability goes with it.

Reducing staff numbers is always hard. What separates the people you keep from the people you let go?

Separations are difficult, but are always based on employees' past ability to get along with co-workers while performing their job effectively. Many companies describe it as "downsizing," IBM has always been known for good management by calling it "right sizing," and I have adopted that terminology. I tend to use normal attrition (moving, children, etc.) by just not rehiring. But it always returns to attitude.

LESSON

As an employee, understand what your leader is looking for in all aspects of your position. As a leader, inform your people what you view as important.

Find It

With so many people looking for employment, you must ensure that your resume stands out. There are seven secrets that will ensure that you are the star that your future employer plucks out of the sky. Remember that the goal of a resume is to get an interview.

1. What is your job objective? You can't scribe before this step. This is your hook, and the statement that most people don't even consider. It is the key that gets you noticed. And always write it from the employer's point of view.

   Self-serving objective: To obtain a responsible (as opposed to irresponsible?) and challenging (what, you don't like dull work?) position where my education and work experience will have valuable application (like finding a cure for cancer?)

Attention-getting objective: Mid-level sales manager where more than 10 years of experience will add value to the sales department and company profits.

Tip: Don't put the word "Objective" next to your objective. Just include your well-stated work target at the beginning of your resume.

2. Companies now scan your resume and will look for key words. Pay close attention to the posting of the job and use the words that have been chosen by the hiring manager. If you use paragraphs, your resume will wind up in the circular file. Choose bullet points for your concise statements. Always use %s, $s, and #s. Percentages, dollar totals, and numbers stand out in the body of a resume.

Incorrect: Was the top sales producer for the region.

Correct: Managed 20 percent of all accounts with sales in excess of $20 million annually.

3. Customize your resume for each company. This will increase your chance of an interview and remember—that is the goal! It's all about personal responsibility and self-leadership for you to find your business success.

4. Read a book about graphic design. Look at ads and pay attention to where you look first. Design is important on your resume! Open space or "white space" is good. Font should be no smaller than 12 point and use Times New Roman or a similar style.

5. Stay upbeat and positive. There is no room for toxic behavior and negative stories. If you don't want an issue with your age,

do not include your year of graduation. Remember this also when listing your positions and companies.

6. Focus only on what is relevant to the job you seek. Leave off irrelevant information such as race, gender, and other personal statistics. Have someone else read and critique your resume with specific examples of why it is good or bad. You are way too close to be objective. Remember to limit the resume to one page!

True story:

While working at GTE Directories, I had the opportunity to review hundreds of resumes. There was one section of the employment application that requested the candidate indicate associations and clubs of which they were members. Two examples that were memorable, but put these folks in the reject pile:

- I belong to AAA—American Automobile Association
- I belong to the Jack LaLanne club (for those of you who don't remember, this is a fitness workout club)

The point is, be very careful on how far you extend your examples!

7. Choose a high-quality 24-pound cream- or white-color paper on which to print your resume. Consider watermarked paper and envelopes. Make sure the envelope is well formatted and the return address is clear, and even check that the stamp is square in the corner. It is all about first impression.

Another inherent part of securing a position is interviewing. Hearing about people who are upset because there are "No jobs out there" or "Poor me, I've been laid off," makes me crazy—so here is my take on the subject.

You've been laid off and have nowhere to go. How is your attitude? Have you become a toxic or difficult person because you are just plain ticked off? Stay on target by considering the following five points:

1. Review the talents you do have and dwell on them.
2. Never berate your old job or boss. It will only come back to haunt you.
3. Be proactive. Post your resume online and stick to it.
4. Realize that you are now in sales and your product is you.
5. Better than 68 percent of people lie on resumes. Don't even think about it.

Example: The human resources department for the job of your dreams has called you. The posting from Monster.com was finally noticed and has paid off. Now what? Do not allow yourself to become a difficult person during the interview. And this does happen! If you are unprepared, you can become negative and aggressive and will undermine your own communications.

From a post on my blog:

> I read your article on Laid Off, Ticked Off and Broke and I have to tell you that I do get it. Can you provide some insight for me? I have 13 years of IT financial mainframe background with a large bank and IBM. During the last several years in my position I was training and re-skilling myself to move into another technical area within the bank but suddenly the bank was downsized. At the time, the area economy was good but I didn't see any interest in me from my local job market. So after my retooling and movement into a new technical arena, my age and experience meet the criteria for outsourcing and downsizing models

being used by the bank and for my sector at the time. Moving the family to India was not an option. In analyzing my skills the mortgage industry looked like a great option even though I know this industry runs in cycles. I did not go into this industry without doing a lot of homework so the company I was with was great and I was mentored for some time and learned a great deal about the business and I can work for them as long as I wish. The issue is I do not have a large enough past client base to support me through this market, so off to the new job market I go. I am open to any suggestions that you may have to offer. Thank you for any assistance.

Here is my response:

In today's market, companies look for talents, not industry experience. Figure out how your talents will benefit any company and write a resume around that. For example: Problem solving, project management, prioritization, conflict resolution, and negotiating. There is always room for great people and I know of companies that are always hiring them! Also, I hear a bit of negativity in your explanation. That needs to be eliminated immediately because the people interviewing have a sixth sense for lack of confidence. Focus on what you bring to the table, not what you are lacking (age, etc.).

Train yourself to be prepared for any interview. In interviews I've had with human resource professionals, they consistently mention how unprepared job seekers are. Here is a quick hit list of five sample questions to get you started and keep you on the right track for the interview. Have a prepared and practiced response ready.

1. Give the single best reason we should consider hiring you over all the others we are considering.
2. If we contact all your previous bosses and/or colleagues, what one trait would they say you could improve? How about a strength?

3. If you could do any job, in any company, what would be the job and name the company?
4. In detail, define strengths, weaknesses, communication style, management style, personality, and values of your ideal boss.
5. What questions would you need me to answer for you to determine if this company and this job is what you are best suited to do?

Take personal responsibility for your success. Learn how to create a great interview.

Stay committed to your decisions, but stay flexible in your approach.

—*Tom Robbins, American novelist*

Ruth Covey, Quality, Security, and Export Control for Armor Designs, is a highly educated engineer and a successful executive with responsibility for research, development, and production. The company is an international leader in the development of next-generation composite materials for armor technologies and products that provide superior protection for individuals, vehicles, and structures. They manufacture a synthetic lightweight alternative to today's conventional armor. Covey went back to Thunderbird School of Management for her Master's in Business Administration to ensure she stayed at the top of her game. Her laser focus has gained her recognition not only in her company but also in her industry.

As a seasoned executive, I knew Covey would provide advice to leaders and employees in understanding why one person may be hired over another. The following list is her guide:

▮ *Accomplishments—whether just graduating from school or with 20 years' experience I want to know what successes the candidate achieved.*
▮ *Education—commensurate with the position being filled.*
▮ *Interpersonal skills—able to interact with others well.*
▮ *Process-oriented—understands that processes are established to accomplish goals and then periodically reviewed for continual improvement.*

Skills that differentiate candidates:

▮ *Detail-oriented—because I'm not.*
▮ *Articulate—ability to clearly and intelligently express oneself in verbal or written communications.*
▮ *Results-oriented—knowing the objective, determining what it takes to reach that objective, and ensuring it is accomplished.*
▮ *Flexible—reaching an objective often requires intelligently adapting to new circumstances, working around obstacles, or ignoring the naysayer.*

LESSON

Think of adapting to your position as adapting to dancing, including the music, tempo, partners, place, and mood.

I hate to even bring this up, but I will: appearance, dress, and posture. Take a look in a full-length mirror and scrutinize these three elements of how your first impression will come across to an interviewer.

1. Appearance: What is the first impression a person will have of you? If you aren't sure, ask 8 to 10 friends, family, or associates. Ask them: "Look at my appearance right now. Would you hire me?" Throw out the high and low comments.
2. Dress: Take the time to determine how others in the company and position in your industry dress. Go on the Internet, stand in front of the business and watch the people coming and going. Check their web site and determine the personality of the web site. Is it formal, suit and tie, and mahogany furniture kind of office or is it informal, jeans, and bring your dog to work kind of environment. And yes, you can tell.
3. Posture: Do you look confident, self-assured, and assertive? Do you display upright and healthy posture? Do you sit on the edge of the chair and look energized and interested? Another hint—spit out the gum, put a pleasant smile on your face or in your voice, extend your hand with a firm handshake, and dump any slang you may use.

Who are you going to believe, me or your own eyes?

—Groucho Marx, American comedian

Keep It

Dave Rawles, author and speaker of Career Workshops, interviewed me for his radio show (KVTT 91.7 FM Radio in Dallas, "The

Truth"). A woman caller wanted to know how, as an administrator, she could help other people who were having problems with the general manager. Currently she was sending them to human resources and nothing was being resolved. Dave, the host of the show, had a wonderful comment. "Human resources is not the ringmaster. Each employee must take personal responsibility for handling their issues except, of course, if the boss's behavior is illegal and crosses EEOC boundaries."

I advised her to suggest different resources to help the employees grow their skills, which in turn will help their confidence in broaching the person directly. I am totally convinced that people want others to "fix" their problems and that most people are too lazy to change their own habits. Don't get pulled into this difficult person behavior. They don't even know they are being a toxic person! Does this sound cruel and abusive? Dave and I agreed that it shouldn't because everyone must take personal responsibility for their own outcomes and choices and leave others to their own devices. In my opinion, if you want to "help" someone, give them considerations instead of ultimatums.

Suggestions:

- Give them a book, web site, or article to read to improve their communications skills. You can help them pave the road to personal development. Do you need to read the same materials?
- Ask them: "How are your negotiation skills? Is it time to take a training class or follow a negotiation guru on a blog?"
- Suggest they find a mentor to help them make different choices and to pass their approaches by another party. Do you have one?

LESSON

Employees are responsible for confronting their own problems and should not expect human resources to fight their battles.

Why do so many skilled people, both employees and leaders, not apply the tools they already have? There are a multitude of reasons but I think it has to do with a person's comfort zone. To be able to focus and use skills on a consistent basis helps you continue to reach the success you deserve. What do you need to improve to keep your job?

What does Matt Leinart have to do with keeping your job? The Arizona Cardinals learned quickly how to take a negative situation and turn it into a positive outcome. In 2004, he was the team's first round draft pick, fueled by his winning the Heisman Trophy presented to the outstanding college football athlete. Enter Kurt Warner to the Cardinals line. He was quickly assigned the starting quarterback by Arizona coach Keith Whisenhunt.

Leinart chose not to mope or become a distraction to the team's success. "It took me a little while just to sit back and say, 'You know what, I can be a distraction. I can be all mad and point the finger and be that guy who is not supportive.' Or I can say, 'I'm going to be a good teammate. I'm going to support Kurt and work my butt off and prepare every day like I'm the starting quarterback,'" Leinart said. His adjusted his attitude because he understands that experience is the best teacher. He thought, "I'm not a bad quarterback. I just happen to be on the same team with this guy, Warner!" He kept his job, stayed focused, and dumped the entitlement attitude.

How can you keep your job if you are a toxic person? I had a courageous e-mail from a reader of my book, *Toxic People*. Just asking this kind of question takes real guts!

Reader: I would say I am a Zipper Lip, as you identified in your book. What should I do?

MPS: This is a behavioral choice you are making to combat a situation that you apparently don't like. The hard reality is that Zipper Lips choose this behavior because they either don't know how else to respond or are too lazy to change. I'm guessing you are in category #1.

Reader: However, I feel people think they are entitled to behave badly. To me bad behavior consists of being too loud, nonstop talking, which most people do and then I never get a chance to talk so I move right into the Zipper Lip behavior.

MPS: Your examples are innate behavioral preferences and you can choose to change them. I had to learn many years ago that everyone doesn't act, communicate, or behave like me. So that means my tolerance has to change toward them because I will never change them. Since most people are too lazy to change, conflict results and bad behavior is displayed. In knowing that, I recommend that you consider learning to be more flexible to other's behaviors and learn how to be an assertive communicator. These actions will help you start to broaden your scope on behaviors, then you can choose what you want to change. Is it hard? You bet. Can it be done? You bet. I'm living proof.

Reader: Toxic people can be anyone who thinks it's OK to break into cars, run red lights, be rude (like run into me in the mall with carts)??

MPS: I believe the only thing we as humans can do is become role models and present our behavior as we expect others to be. You'll be amazed the impact this change in thinking has.

LESSON

If you whine and moan about other people's behavior, you identify yourself as a toxic person, and you will have a difficult time keeping your job.

The No-No List

■ Don't have an affair (that means sex) with anyone associated with your work, including a vendor, boss, or colleague. Even in a great economy, it becomes a strike against you and it rarely, if ever, turns out well.

■ Don't post anything on the Internet that you don't want your mom to see. Companies do check, even if they say they don't because of privacy issues.

■ Don't get yourself into a financial jam. Companies will check your FICO™ (Fair Isaac Company) credit score to see if you are worthy of a promotion, or even remaining on the job. If you are already there, put on your big boy or big girl pants and do something about it.

- Don't ever attend a meeting unprepared. This is instant death, because your competition will always be willing and ready to take your glory.
- Don't gossip or get involved in office politics. I know you've heard it before but if you still do it, stop.
- Don't let what the chattering classes say bother you. This includes your "frenemies," pundits, and press. Don't take it personally if they do.
- Don't hang out with negative people, downers, or victims. Their goal is to make you as miserable as they are.
- Don't let your career happen to you. Don't wait for anyone to suggest a job, or offer you a raise, or find you the next great job.
- Don't get stressed and out of balance. Train yourself to take care of yourself first because you can't respond if you are crazed.
- Don't ever do anything unethical and vaccinate yourself against moral amnesia.

Love It

Choose a job you love, and you will never have to work a day in your life.

—Confucius, Chinese thinker and social philosopher

You have to get strong by defeating bad choices. Sure we have all worked for difficult bosses and have said, "I can't hack it." This sets a defeatist mind-set and builds a barrier to ever loving your job. The nurtured sense of helplessness feeds the emotional vampires skulking in the dark corners of your brain. The question is, how do you jump-start your ambition and love the job you have in this very moment? Layer in gossip, office politics, and jerks at work and it can be hard to love your job. My recommendation is to find part of your job that you do enjoy and focus on that.

I interviewed Doug Ducey, Chairman of the Board for iMemories, because he has the proven ability to build a successful high-growth consumer brand through his people. He was the CEO of Cold Stone Creamery and has great insight on employees and leaders. I asked him what sort of skills he looks for when he identifies leaders and stars.

- *They must be able to stand on their own two feet.*
- *They must know how to flatten any potholes or speed bumps.*
- *I expect them to ask themselves, "What more can I contribute?"*
- *Number one concern is how they treat the customer.*
- *Do their job and supply information.*
- *Must be smart and a cultural fit. Don't pull the "I'm smarter than you."*
- *Must think results not activities (how hard the person works).*
- *They must understand core values and be able to recite them.*

Ducey's formula: *core values + leadership + culture = success.* Ducey stated that core values give employees something to be accountable for, along with the vision. The employees should be able to recite the core values without thinking, which guides every activity and becomes an internal compass.

And this was my favorite comment by Ducey: "During any meeting the boss should always speak last and if asked their opinion as other people are speaking, they should answer by saying, 'I don't know enough yet.'" Ducey suggested that the person at the meeting with the least amount of importance speak first because this technique allows people to bring up their best thinking.

If you are the leader of the group, try this. If you are not the boss or leader, suggest it and you will get a star in the crown of success.

LESSON

Stick to your core values, know the same for your company, and apply the tactics of successful communications.

Whatever you are, be a good one.

—*Abraham Lincoln, U.S. President*

Empower Yourself: Dump the Entitlement Attitude

Tired of the endless stream of negativity, stress, and confusion created by chaos? I don't care if you're talking about the economy, job, boss, colleague, or anything else in your environment. Thriving in chaos is a decision not to get sucked into a negative spiral. The choice is personal responsibility. Here are 10 considerations that are vital to thriving in chaos:

1. Communication. Paraphrase to clarify what you hear. Never try to read between the lines or guess a person's intent. Ask questions and continue to delve into the topic. Make your conversations less about you and more about them.

2. Flexibility. You have to be ready at a moment's notice to shift your thinking and stay open to change. Continue to grow your skills, ask for additional assignments, question everything, and be prepared. Example: Do you have the mind-set to move on and find another job if your job was eliminated? If you do, congratulations, you are a flexible thinker.

3. Empowerment. Empower yourself and dump the entitlement attitude. Nobody owes you anything, either at work or at home. You do owe it to yourself to be accountable for every choice and every outcome.

Laziness may appear attractive, but work gives satisfaction.

—Anne Frank, Holocaust victim

4. Responsiveness. Learn to respond quickly to changes in your company and the work you do there. Reacting is simply knee jerking, while responding involves using learned skills that help you to make decisions more quickly. Don't waste time and energy complaining.

5. Learning. Support and promote lifelong learning. Train yourself to be a learner by using downloads, books on tape, and

other resources. Read diverse resources and listen to news from a variety of media outlets. Engage your work group in educational activities.

> *I wish there was a knob on the TV to turn up the intelligence. There's a knob called "brightness," but it doesn't work.*
>
> —*Unknown*

6. Innovate. Find different and better ways to solve problems. Learn how to use the Internet to find books and other resources on innovation and how to stimulate creativity in the workplace.

> *Every day we're saying, "How can we keep this customer happy?" How can we get ahead in innovation by doing this, because if we don't, somebody else will.*
>
> —*Bill Gates, American entrepreneur and founder of Microsoft*

7. Cutting back. Always look for ways to reduce spending, such as trimming travel expenses and entertainment costs. If you don't know much about your organization's financials, ask. You may learn something that enables you to brainstorm a solution that makes your firm more profitable.
8. Energy. Stay enthusiastic and forward thinking. Make the work environment fun and exciting. Allow negative

discussion, but learn how to respond with, "What is the worst thing that can happen?"

9. Accountability. Be a role model for others by taking responsibility for every decision you make. Know that you always have three choices: take it, leave it, or change it. And challenge yourself by asking, "So, what's the plan?"

10. Goals. Understand your personal goals and those of your organization. You will not be able to thrive in chaos if you have no idea where you are going. Find a system that works for you and stay on track. It is your job!

We must walk consciously only part way toward our goal, and then leap in the dark to our success.

—*Henry David Thoreau, American essayist and philosopher*

Life After Layoff

I've known Marlys Foster, a Mary Kay consultant, for several years and I remember her espousing the love for her job and company. So I was surprised when I received an e-mail explaining that she had been laid off after almost three decades with Principal Financial. I am happy to report she is now an Independent Beauty Consultant with Mary Kay. She shared some her layoff revelations from this unexpected action from her company.

Foster shared a detailed list of her experience:
■ *Financial experts tell you to have emergency funds for four to five months available at all times. I see their advice has much wisdom.*

■ *I saw the layoff coming, but our department and business unit was doing well. I briefly thought about it when the company announced that they were looking for ways to reduce expenses. I dismissed those thoughts because of the ROE (Return on Equity) for our business unit.*

■ *Although by employment law, the company had to give us a demographic breakdown by title and age, there were no names on the list. After working in a company for a time, you have built relationships and a professional network. (See the last chapter on why you should use a personal e-mail address.)*

■ *There was a buzz around Des Moines that Principal was laying-off people two days before the actual announcements. This historically has been and has the necessity to be a strictly confidential matter . . . where is the source of information sharing and what else do others outside the company know that the employees have not been told?*

■ *Layoffs affect the ones left behind also: more work, reassignments, guilt, worry, loss of trust of management, insecurity, and loss of production due to more watercooler or e-mail chatter about the situation. The ones left behind have to go through the "grief" process also to name the emotions, worries, concerns, and work through them.*

■ *When a layoff is so large, it cannot and should not be taken personally. It is an excellent time to reflect on your value through your skills, strengths, experiences, and accomplishments. It is an excellent time to reflect on your challenges, weaknesses, and what you can do about them.*

■ *Admit that when you were in the meeting with the announcement of termination/layoff that you probably didn't hear all the details from the HR representative. Read and reread the fine print of the release and waiver paperwork, get advice from an attorney, get advice from your financial advisor and your tax person and/or accountant. Tell people what you need from them. Write your questions down, ask reliable sources, get your answers in writing whenever possible, and always keep the name, telephone number of the person, and date you were given the information. Confirm what you understand about your questions by restating what you understand. Documentation will be your best friend if there are problems later.*

LESSON

Be prepared for the good and the bad. Read between the lines for your industry, and your company.

Getting fired is nature's way to telling you that you had the wrong job in the first place.

—Hal Lancaster, Wall Street Journal

On top of being laid off:

▌ It's better than staying in a job you don't like.
▌ It frees up your future to do what you really want, like turning a hobby into a career.
▌ It's a good time for reflection on your skills, your wants, your needs.
▌ It forces you to cut out all the worthless extra stuff you buy.

- It makes you think outside the employment box and your experience. Education, health care, law, and energy industries are being touted as the growth industries.
- It teaches you that you must move fast and respond quickly to real opportunity and also to your intuition.
- It teaches you to spend your days pounding the pavement and your nights surfing the Internet.
- It forces you to be humble and to can the ego because you will probably be making less than you were before.
- It means that you may be working for someone younger than you.
- It lets you expand your geographic boundaries and helps you see the positive side of moving to a new city.
- It lets you think of being laid off as a savvy sabbatical—so use the time wisely.

Ralph had worked for the company for 22 years. He had done well, had a respectable 401(k), bought a new boat, and was satisfied with his success. With a snap decision from the leaders of the company, Ralph's division was closed and he was laid off. In his length of employment, he had never taken a "long" vacation, so decided to treat himself to some well-deserved vacation. He knew his severance package would provide even more cushion. Ralph had the BTO attitude . . . Big Time Operator.

A month quickly passed, and another, and another. He confidently told friends and family that he was well connected and could get a job anytime he wanted. He blew threw his savings and realized he was in a difficult position with no job, no money, and creditors calling him daily. He started borrowing from everyone he knew, lied to everyone about his situation, and found himself in a real jam.

After being evicted from his apartment, he knew he was at the end of his rope. Ralph was now in hiding.

How to eliminate the "Ralph Factor":

■ Be prepared for the unexpected. This includes keeping your business network updated along with your resume.

■ If you are laid off, begin looking for your next position immediately.

■ Have a financial reserve and use it wisely. It's not vacation money.

■ Eliminate all superfluous spending and let everyone in your circle know that you are in the "frugal" state.

■ Don't borrow money from friends and family. You will only ruin relationships.

■ Keep your credit cards paid off. They won't become a problem if you are laid off.

■ If you have children, start early by showing them how the household money is earned and spent. When there is an emergency, let them in on the changes that must be made.

■ Keep open communication with your partner—on everything. Surprises only breed conflict.

You have homework to do. Don't just read the ideas in this chapter. Find your Achilles heel in your position today and take action. This will save you grief, hardship, and conflict later on. Karen Young, my stepdaughter, has the right attitude when she says, "If I get laid off one more time, I can retire." How about you?

CHAPTER 10

Preach It, Teach It

...

Control, Decisions, Money, and Parenting

Do you have people in your life to whom you preach because you want them to take personal responsibility for their decisions? Do you also take the time to *teach* them how to do what you're instructing? I believe that everyone must be accountable in helping others be more responsible.

Now—is that little voice in your head screaming, "But you said I can't change other people!" Well, you are right about that. What you *can* do, however, is act as a role model to others, and lead them to better decision making through the example of your actions. In fact, the common thread that I weave through the interviews in this book is the solid fact of taking responsibility and believing in yourself.

My husband Al and I had the pleasure of taking our wonderful young friend Christian to a local banquet and silent auction. Upon entering the auction hall, I immediately fell in love with a carved wooden bear. Ever the generous friend, Christian texted his mom and asked her to let him know what the balance on his debit card was. Once he found out that he had enough to make an offer, he began his bidding and won the bear; and so, I am now the proud owner of this "Beeso Bear." Christian is developing fiscal, relationship, and personal responsibility for his decisions—and all at the ripe age of 12. Playing an active part in his constructive development is wonderful. Our goal is to share experiences through our actions, and help others learn successful life habits. Christian's mom is also serving as a great preacher and teacher.

Consider to whom *you* might have the opportunity to teach personal responsibility. How can you help someone at work free herself from her "entitlement attitude"? Do you need to start with yourself? One of the goals of this book is to provide an insider's view of what people who have decided to take personal responsibility for their outcomes do in their daily actions, and what actions they take when negative business situations hit. Be ready to flex your attention and actions, no matter what the economy may do.

The common threads are clear. My challenge for you is to find the messages that resonate with you and your particular situation, and to ultimately convert these messages into action. Many leaders I talked to discussed how doing the right thing is related to success, being a star, getting promoted, and living the life of your dreams. Other leaders gave us a thoughtful focus on managing excellence.

Excellence is not a singular act, but a habit. You are what you repeatedly do.

— *Shaquille O'Neal, American professional basketball player*

Rod Covey, Executive Director of the Center for Leadership Excellence Peace Officer Standards and Training Board at the Department of Public Safety, is the epitome of a dedicated public servant. He teaches leadership excellence within the ranks of police departments throughout the United States. I asked Covey to share an example of a time when he was determined to change a negative into a positive, and how he was able to respond—not react—to a difficult position in business.

Covey responded with the following story:

We have had an excellent relationship with a local resort that we used as a venue for meetings and training. They had been great hosts for two years; and then when the economy went south and they needed our business the most, we were forced to abandon them. I did not want to burn any bridges; but we clearly didn't need to be at the wrong hotel at the wrong time. AIG and others took a beating over this very issue; the company had just received a large sum of money as part of the bailout, and yet here they were at a posh resort hosting a meeting. No explanation that their company leader seemed to offer mattered; the damage was done. We didn't want to be under this microscope and were trying to avoid that kind of embarrassing press, because the government surely wasn't going to bail us out if we lost our funding.

Another point regarding this topic, from a state government perspective: I think that when the economy goes in the tank (which it's done it three times in my 32-year career with Department of Public Safety), it gives leaders in government the opportunity to reevaluate what they are doing and to look carefully at every part of their organization. We must take responsibility for the answers to these questions:

What are we currently doing that is not part of our primary mission?

What are we doing that we are not mandated to do?

What are we doing that someone else is—or should be—doing?

LESSON

If we didn't have down times, we would never be forced to look at the efficiency and effectiveness in our operations.

Covey continued:

It is difficult to ask for more money, people, and resources unless you are sure that you have made the best possible use of what you currently have. Yet leaders and employees do that all of the time. They ask for more, and if the economy is good, the justification for more becomes less important. That is how some government organizations have become bloated. There are great people working in city, county, state, and federal government; but there are also a lot of people that could not survive in private industry where they would have to produce on a daily basis.

LESSON

Make the tough decisions. They are noticed.

Dr. Geoff Haw, Managing Director of Sagacity Services, Australia, says:

I am convinced that an exacerbating factor in all this financial downturn is the overwhelming infiltration of negativity in the market place.

"It seems to me that there are four main choices any small business owner/manager can make in the light of challenging times for business:

1. *Concede defeat and close down.*
2. *"Pull the horns in," and* trim back—*staffing levels, stock levels, production levels—and tragically, reducing marketing at a time when it is probably more needed than ever.*
3. *Adopt a stringent review of the efficiency of the business, trimming all fat and working on a lean operating strategy, but trying to maintain the current levels of business. A more persuasive marketing strategy may be required to keep sales up, so that has to be a marriage of return on investment in marketing, that is, what works and represents value for money?*
4. *Decide to take a calculated risk by looking for new opportunities that could come from the difficult times, those that may have some synergy with the business, and set up some new enterprise, product, or system.*

LESSON

Self-examination and the right philosophy are the most critical factors for success, especially in difficult times.

The trend can be very positive when you're looking at lessons learned. Many times, however, I believe that the focus remains on the negative downturn that is constantly headlined in the news. If you get stuck with the masses complaining about issues you can't control, one thing is for sure: you will only validate the negativity that is permeating the minds of many. So stop today. Allow your mind to take a breather—and start looking for your silver lining.

Life is hard, and oftentimes very unfair; but I do believe in the power of attraction, that is, that you will attract how you think and act. It's a simple notion, really, so learn from the experts; or better yet, become an expert. In his book *Outliners: The Story of Success*, author Malcolm Gladwell focuses on some interesting research. In Chapter 2: *The 10,000-hour rule*, Gladwell quotes a study validating that the magic number for anyone—including you—to become a true expert on a topic is 10,000 hours spent on that task. Neurologist Daniel Levitin said, "The emerging picture from such studies is that ten thousand hours of practice is required to achieve the level of mastery associated with being a world-class expert—in anything." From Bill Gates to the Beatles, the examples seem to prove this theory. I find this information truly captivating, and have come to realize that genuine, learned expertise paves the road from preaching to teaching.

Michael Austin, Chief Executive Officer and President of Armor Sports Holdings, has held key leadership roles in manufacturing and distribution companies in small business and Fortune 500 environments. He also has broad industry experience that ranges from sports medical products, lightning location, data distribution, and aerospace. In our interview, I asked Michael for an example of how he and his companies have turned a negative business situation around. His answer is insightful and very creative! (By the way: Armor Sports Holdings is not related to Armor Designs and Ruth Covey!)

Austin's reply:

Last year, we transitioned Armor Sports from an operating company to a licensing company. So rather than manufacturing, sales, and marketing, we are only providing tech support to a company in Texas who is doing all the work we used to do. Consequently, we completely downsized our business. This was a decision that we made before the big and sudden decline in the economy, and was actually part of our business plan.

Having successfully accomplished the transition, my dilemma was moving on to the next project in the current environment. We are a small business with single-digit market share in a market segment dominated by six major players. Our annual revenue was less than any one of our competitors' marketing budgets. So we decided to expand market penetration and reduce our cost by licensing the technology to our largest distributor. As a result, the product continues to increase in market recognition and overall volume—and at a reduced cost.

LESSON

Be ready for the unexpected—it may come in a small package.

Professional associations are currently being forced to make some difficult decisions concerning their positioning and strategizing for success—and how they plan to survive during trying economic times. I believe that now more than ever, professional memberships are important to solve problems, develop income, and learn what other people are doing. As a professional speaker, I do a good portion of my speaking for these kinds of organizations and their members. Therefore, I asked Executive Director of the National Speakers Association Stacy Tetschner for his input on how my professional association is responding to negatives happening today. As these groups gather the information and preach about cost savings, they also conduct seminars in a variety of forums to share survival techniques for the speaking industries' participants.

Stacy explained:

The National Speakers Association has been constantly reevaluating expenses to ensure that we are spending our members' money prudently, and that they are getting the best return for their investment. Nothing is a sacred cow, and we are implementing changes from staffing to fast-tracking some "green" ideas that can save us money.

We also realize that these tough times are not just tough for us, but also for our members. With decreased cash flow, some of the speakers are making daunting decisions as to whether they can make the investment in their dues this year. So for those who would not be able to pay the full amount up front, we are offering a quarterly or bi-annually payment option. This allows them to stay connected to their professional community during the times when they likely need it the most.

Regarding staffing, there are two things upon which we have specifically focused:

1. *Whenever someone leaves their position, the vacancy is reevaluated to see if we can redistribute the work to the existing staff team and to ensure that what they were doing was truly adding to the value we provide our members. We hire for attitude and train for skills, so when we redistribute work, we know we already have the people with the right attitude on board. We then try to build positions around them that take advantage of their skills and passions so we can get the very best from them. In addition to getting the most out of our resources, this causes employees to truly love working here.*

2. *When it comes to the hard decision of having to let people go because of expenses, we look to see if there are ways to reduce everyone's hours a little bit instead of totally eliminating one position. When we have the right mix of people on board, we want to keep them all; and everyone hates to see someone get laid off. In some cases, we have had full-time people that wanted to move to part time because of a family situation; and we were again able to redistribute how the work gets done to accommodate everyone—and keep everyone employed.*

Because of the information provided by NSA, I understand the importance of including webinars, teleseminars, and articles to my clients when they book me to present keynotes and workshops. NSA has also awarded me with the Certified Speaking Professional (CSP) designation held by less that 10 percent of the speakers in the world. Everything I can do as a speaker to differentiate myself from the crowd adds value for my clients.

LESSON

Use the expertise of the team to determine ways to improve the bottom line. Hire for attitude; train for skill.

Dale Irvin is the world's only Professional Summarizer. He attends meetings, pays attention to every word spoken by every speaker, and notices every detail of the event. Then, throughout the day, he will "summarize" the event with a comedy monologue written on the spot. In compiling this book, I thought it important to include insight from someone who knows how to lighten up. Even with very serious topics, Dale teaches people how to laugh at themselves and the situation.

Dale's Laughter Stimulus Package:

When times are particularly difficult—no matter what those difficulties are—the best remedy is to add more laughter. I am totally serious here. Laughter is one of the few things we do that not only feels and is good for us, but is free. There is no charge for laughter. There is no tax (yet), and there is no license required. You can laugh as much as you want in any 24-hour period—and it will not cost you a cent. Other than air, there is no other offer like this on the planet. You could literally laugh from the time you wake up until the time you go to bed and you won't even have to dip into the change on your nightstand. It's a beautiful thing, and one that we don't use to our full advantage.

LESSON

Laughing doesn't cost anything; so simply lighten up.

"Nothing is more annoying than those who stand for nothing," Penny Barrington Haw, Coach and Trainer for Capacity Life Coaching said. I met Penny Barrington Haw many years ago when I was speaking in Australia. Penny teaches people how to fulfill their life dreams, and uses her training and intellect to help people. She not only preaches what she knows, but also shows others how to become a role model for everyone they touch.

I asked Penny how she sees people react in business today, and she responded:

Reactions in business are going to depend on how long you have been in business, what your line is, and how much leeway you have financially. Somewhere in there, business reactions are the same as personal reactions—because businesspeople never stop being human:

- *Own your actions—in other words, choose how you respond. Start looking for opportunities to expand or direct the niche to produce new products. Think creatively and contemplate strategic alliances.*
- *Start creating. Diversify without detracting from the niche.*
- *Do not get worried about time limits. Keep pressing on.*
- *Do not align or base your self-worth or self-value on money, or how much you have. In the end, it's relationships that matter.*
- *Stay healthy and never let stress overtake you.*
- *Remember that resilience and self-worth are critical.*
- *Be sensible and do not react on the rebound or in desperation. Give ideas and thoughts time to grow and take effect.*
- *Increase your customer service because these relationships are what build your business.*
- *Use any downtime (if you can keep going financially) to de-clutter. Tidy up. Off-load. Take a "make room for new things" approach.*
- *Do what you can to feel hopeful. Hopelessness is tough to deal with, especially when the source of this feeling appears to be very real. Determine who your friends are—the ones who will love you, rich or poor—because they can be a source of self-value.*
- *If you are doing OK, get going and do even better. When you can, help someone else.*
- *Keep in mind that no matter how bad things may seem, people will not be squirreling away their money forever—especially Generation Y. They may be our saviors, because they seem freer to believe in the future no matter what.*

LESSON

One person's solution is another's confusion. So choose your actions wisely and don't knee jerk.

Kelly Zitlow, Vice President of Suburban Mortgage, has seen the ups and downs of the market. I was pleased when she agreed to answer my question concerning how she and her company were responding in a difficult market. Zitlow responded:

As a manager in the financial industry today, I see fear in the eyes of my employees on daily basis. This is a daunting vision, one that I try to tackle the only way I know how: with motivation, leadership, and by never letting them see fear in my eyes. I am optimistic but sincere about the realities of our business. Being in a financial services industry, we can't tune out the devastating headlines; we actually must follow them, digest the information, and be sure we are staying current on all of the factors affecting our business. My goal each and every day is to help my staff focus on the things we can control instead of the multitude of things we can't. We can change and adapt to the industry today; we can control our actions and our thoughts; we can control the level of service we give to our clients. I also make sure they know I have confidence in them, and that despite the recent challenges, we can make it through this difficult time—and we will!

LESSON

Focus on what you can control, not on what you can't control.

Entrepreneurs John and Anne Draper left their executive corporate positions several years ago, and because of their love for the outdoors, purchased a 10,000-acre ranch in Colorado. Armed with years preaching in their respective careers, they are now able to teach the ranch employees—and at the same time, learn for themselves—about how to operate a successful ranch.

During my interview with the Drapers, they shared wonderful insights in how they were responding in current trying times. Their responses:

> *Our recreational business offers a small, remote mountain lodge available for family/business retreats—with just about every kind of outdoor event available in Colorado. Our business survives in a highly competitive field purely on the discretionary income of its customers. Because of these troubled economic times, we reassessed our business and marketing plans. And so we took the following actions:*
>
> ∎ *Increased our marketing efforts, and expanded our product line.*
> ∎ *Concentrated on media and venues that have been successful in the past.*
> ∎ *Explored new and creative outlets, such as various Internet forums and new international target markets.*
> ∎ *Stepped up efforts to sell other products, sell packaged meat, and attract weddings and corporate retreats.*
> ∎ *Prepared to discount our prices as necessary.*
> ∎ *Deferred capital expenditures and, because a large part of our expenses are fixed, we are focusing on those cost savings that will benefit us today and beyond.*

LESSON

Be nimble and prudent while increasing spending to maximize success in the moment.

Executive Allan Zinky, PMP Director of American Express Technologies, shared a wonderful—and timely—story with me about his sister. I know of people who have been evicted from their homes recently, and who have reacted in a way that created an even more untenable result. This example is a huge lesson on how to turn a devastating situation into a beneficial one.

Upon asking Allan my interview question—a negative situation that has had a positive ending—he was quick to respond with the following:

> *My sister recently was notified that she was three months behind on her Home Owners Association (HOA) dues. In October, she learned that she was being evicted from her leased house, because her California landlord was in foreclosure. She seized the situation and turned it into an opportunity by attending the home auction and purchasing the house she was leasing well under the market value. My sister had already spent time and money moving out. She moved back in—and now is the proud owner of the house.*

LESSON

Take risk, move swiftly, and believe in a positive outcome.

Money Mastery

Controlling finances seems to be a major issue for most people—whether the economy is up or down. Do you preach the importance of saving and spending prudently? Have you taught yourself how to develop money mastery? You can't teach others this learned skill if you don't do it yourself.

I believe that an underlying reason for individual financial problems is that people react to a purchase impulse, rather than logically responding to a need. This is why the end caps in retail and grocery stores are sold to manufacturers at a premium; it follows the psychology of how we buy. You see something you didn't even need, you find it appealing, and you react—and snap it up. It had not been on your radar, but you purchase it anyway. The real mystery here is—how do we stop the spending insanity? One word: discipline!

You must learn to respond positively to purchases and money. Follow these simple rules—and you can be in control. Remember: it's all about your spending habits, and the only person who can control the money in your life is *you*. Here is my short list:

- Write down what you earn on a monthly basis.
- Subtract all your expenditures and include everything. (If you don't know, keep a piece of paper with you and every time you spend any money, make a quick note, and include the cash you use.)
- You can spend whatever is leftover from this.
- Always know what your credit score is.

I'm spending a year dead for tax reasons.

—*Douglas Adams, British comic writer*

Your credit score is more important now than ever. Companies *do* check it before hiring or promoting employees. In addition, if you aren't careful about your credit, you could end up paying dearly for a low credit score. Not only can a low score stand in the way of getting a loan for your dream home or car, but even if you do get the loan, a less-than-stellar score will make it all the more expensive. As your credit score decreases, you become more of a credit risk in the eyes of lenders. This means that they'll attach a higher interest rate to your loan, and your monthly payments will jump. On the other hand, a high score will *lower* that interest rate.

Credit scores can range from a high of 850 to a low of 300. Of course, the higher the score, the more likely you are to get a great interest rate and approval for a loan. And consider the impression that you make with an employer if he or she checks your credit. In a tight employment market, every piece of the puzzle becomes important. How do *you* rank?

- 700 or above—Excellent to Very Good; your rates will be even better.
- 680 to 699—Good; but you won't get offered the lowest interest rates.
- 620 to 679—OK; but you will definitely not have the best terms.
- 580 to 619—Low; your loan will definitely be more expensive in terms of interest.
- 500 to 580—Poor; you will only be able to get a specialized type of secured loan tailored to people with bad credit.

How might this play out in terms of an employment situation? Well, let's say that you are up for a position that seems like a great fit. You have a credit score of 608, and your competing peer has a credit score of 705. If you were the hiring manager, whom would you choose? Remember that companies want to hire and promote people who take personal responsibility for their actions—including how you manage your finances.

> *Before you speak, listen. Before you write, think. Before you spend, earn. Before you invest, investigate. Before you criticize, wait. Before you pray, forgive. Before you quit, try. Before you retire, save. Before you die, give.*
>
> —*William Arthur Ward, American scholar, author, editor, pastor, and teacher*

Here are eight tips on how to get out of the Financial Failure Pit:

1. Get more plastic, making your new cards debit only. If you don't have the money on a card, you can't spend it.
2. Cut up your credit cards. Right now.
3. Focus on "Drive By's"—drive by the mall, drive by your favorite store, and drive home. If you're not there, you can't spend.
4. Shop with a list. If it's not on the list, you don't buy it.
5. If you see something you "have to have," look at it, touch it, then walk away. Give yourself 24 hours to determine if this is the best way to spend your money.
6. Start saving. Get on board with your employers' saving plans or whatever is appropriate. Do you really think Social Security will be around when you retire?

7. When you do purchase, comparison shop, whether in person or online.
8. Use the 20 percent rule. Your total debt load—except for your mortgage payment—should not exceed 20 percent of your yearly after-tax income.

A Word on Parenting . . .

Although I have not raised children myself, I became a wife, mother, and grandmother the day I married Al. I made a choice at 20 years old not to have children. My family was not the most functional in the world and I didn't feel that I had the best foundation and experience upon which to build my own family. That said, I am an excellent observer and have noticed that for the last 20 years or so, many parents are not building a platform of personal responsibility for their kids. This creates youngsters and adults who don't truly understand how the real world works.

If you are a parent, be the person you want your child or children to be. Here is the "Marsha Quick Start" parenting guide:

- Be honest and open. Talk to your kids about drugs, sex, and other uncomfortable but incredibly important issues.
- Be an active participant in your teen's life. Know your child's interests.
- Think "harm reduction," not zero tolerance. They *will* experiment in certain areas; it's up to you to decide how to address this.
- Don't believe everything you read or hear. Open communication will solve most problems that you and your child face.

- Show an authoritative (not authoritarian) parenting style, which involves a combination of warmth and firmness.
- Set high standards and have high expectations for your teens regarding their behavior. Enforce these standards with consistent discipline.
- Monitor your child's behavior simply by being present (before and after they go out, for example) and asking a few simple questions in a neutral, nonaccusatory tone.
- Actively attempt to build in genuine, positive interactions throughout the day or week. If there is a problem, let your son or daughter know that you are unhappy with their *behavior*—and not with them as a person.
- Encourage your youngster to be involved in extracurricular activities.
- Address abusive language. It is a powerful means by which teens control the actions of others—including dating partners, parents, and peers.

If you are going to preach to other people about anything, you need to follow the same rules yourself—just like everything else we've discussed in this book. My question for you is: what have we discussed that has really resonated with you? What did you read that gave you an "A-ha" moment, and that will help you be better at managing your life and work? What is the one idea that will move you from a negative situation to a positive one?

Review the chapters now, and pinpoint exactly what you want to change. Remember to allow yourself to quit while you're behind. It's OK to scale back your original goal; just choose a different goal in a similar area, or find a completely new goal. Allow yourself flexibility.

If at first you don't succeed, before you try again, stop to figure out what you did wrong.

—*Leo Rosten, Polish-born U.S. author*

The one hot idea on which I will focus from *The Reactor Factor* is:

_____

_____

Now get busy. Go annoy people—take personal responsibility.

52 Lessons Learned

Recommendation: With 52 lessons, focus on one lesson each week of the year. This will help you respond instead of react to the negatives that can permeate your business life and hold you from the success you deserve. The Chapter numbers are included so you can turn directly to the information most important for you.

1. Lesson: Do what you should, not what you can. (Chapter 1)
2. Lesson: Make disruptive decisions and stay on task. (Chapter 1)
3. Lesson: Stay lean and mean and focus on your customer. (Chapter 1)
4. Lesson: The most important thing you can do for your clients is stay in business. (Chapter 2)
5. Lesson: Change or suffer the consequences. (Chapter 2)
6. Lesson: Respond to a situation by seeking advice from professionals when needed and don't react if the answer isn't what you wanted to hear. (Chapter 3)
7. Lesson: Don't try to control the uncontrollable. (Chapter 3)
8. Lesson: Choose to respond to the situation, be assertive, and start a conversation. (Chapter 3)
9. Lesson: Tune up your attitude. (Chapter 3)
10. Lesson: Be specific when you outline the criteria you expect people to bring to your team. (Chapter 4)

11. Lesson: Remember the three Cs: Commitment, contribution, and communications. (Chapter 4)
12. Lesson: Simplify, act, document. (Chapter 4)
13. Lesson: Know what traits are important to the leader. (Chapter 4)
14. Lesson: Know what you expect with employees, peers, and teammates. Don't waver from your focus and your needs. It will help you keep the business healthy. (Chapter 4)
15. Lesson: An absolute priority should be exceptional customer service in securing a satisfied client base and energized employees. (Chapter 4)
16. Lesson: Establish solid core values then eat, live, and breathe them. (Chapter 4)
17. Lesson: Fit people are warriors in life; they have mastered themselves. (Chapter 5)
18. Lesson: There is a perception of people who are overweight, whether it is right or wrong. This is your life and you are on center stage. (Chapter 5)
19. Lesson: What kind of culture are you creating? You are 100 percent responsible for how you handle workplace infections. (Chapter 6)
20. Lesson: You can turn a 23-foot speedboat on a dime but it takes a lot to get that cruise ship turned around! (Chapter 6)
21. Lesson: Fine-tune everything and use constant communication to keep your group informed. (Chapter 6)
22. Lesson: During good times and bad, communication maintains creativity, boosts morale, and creates a positive environment. (Chapter 6)
23. Lesson: Network with a purpose to create visibility for you and your company. (Chapter 6)

24. Lesson: Learn about social networking or better yet, hire someone who can help you take advantage of everything available. (Chapter 7)
25. Lesson: What social networking group could you form? Create your own fan club. Be original and imaginative. (Chapter 7)
26. Lesson: Change your habits of sending your messages by using new methods and social networks. (Chapter 7)
27. Lesson: You are entitled to opportunity. (Chapter 8)
28. Lesson: Determine what you can do to succeed. How do you become a Star? (Chapter 8)
29. Lesson: In today's competitive job market, you must know what you know and understand the benefit of your skills for the company you are interviewing with or work for. (Chapter 8)
30. Lesson: Be deliberate and premeditated in your mental processing. (Chapter 8)
31. Lesson: Dress appropriately (and you thought dress was no longer important!). (Chapter 8)
32. Lesson: Challenge your own thinking. If you don't, someone else will! (Chapter 8)
33. Lesson: It's all about tuning up your attitude and tuning in your communications. Dump the entitlement attitude. (Chapter 8)
34. Lesson: The key to a good business is in developing personal relationships, do not prejudge anyone, and treat everyone fairly. (Chapter 9)
35. Lesson: As an employee, understand what your leader is looking for in all aspects of your position. As a leader, inform your people what you view as important. (Chapter 9)

36. Lesson: Define your job as to whom you serve versus who you have authority over. (Chapter 9)
37. Lesson: Think of adapting to your position as adapting to dancing, including the music, tempo, partners, place, and mood. (Chapter 9)
38. Lesson: Employees are responsible for confronting their own problems and should not expect human resources to fight their battles. (Chapter 9)
39. Lesson: If you whine and moan about other people's behavior, you identify yourself as a toxic person, and you will have a difficult time keeping your job. (Chapter 9)
40. Lesson: Stick to your core values, know the same for your company, and apply the tactics of successful communications.
41. Lesson: Be prepared for the good and the bad. Read between the lines for your industry and your company. (Chapter 9)
42. Lesson: If we didn't have downtimes, we would never be forced to look at the efficiency and effectiveness in our operations. (Chapter 10)
43. Lesson: Make the tough decisions. They are noticed. (Chapter 10)
44. Lesson: Self-examination and the right philosophy are the most critical factors for success, especially in difficult times. (Chapter 10)
45. Lesson: Focus on the unexpected—it may come in a small package. (Chapter 10)
46. Lesson: To succeed, you cannot be afraid or hesitant to stand up and lead. (Chapter 10)

47. Lesson: Use the expertise of the team to determine ways to improve the bottom line. Hire for attitude, train for skill. (Chapter 10)
48. Lesson: Laughing doesn't cost anything so simply lighten up. (Chapter 10)
49. Lesson: One person's solution is another's confusion. So choose your actions wisely and don't knee jerk. (Chapter 10)
50. Lesson: Focus on what you can control, not on what you can't control. (Chapter 10)
51. Lesson: Be nimble and prudent while increasing spending to maximize success in the moment. (Chapter 10)
52. Lesson: Take risk, move swiftly, and believe in a positive outcome. (Chapter 10)

Please e-mail me to receive this list in a PDF format so you can share it with the people you work with who really need it. After all, you read the book and they didn't: mps@marshapetriesue.com

Selections from *The Reactor Factor* are also available as an application for iPhone and iPod touch. Powered by Tapstack, you can flip through 60 cards with messages that will help you stay focused and handle difficult work situations without going nuclear. Check the app store in iTunes or from your device to download *The Reactor Factor Tapstack* today. Questions? Visit www.MarshaPetrie Sue.com.

A true friend is someone who thinks that you are a good egg even though he knows that you are slightly cracked.

—Bernard Meltzer, radio host

APPENDIX

Connections

■ ■ ■

Professionals Highlighted in this Book

■ Todd Davis, LifeLock
www.lifelock.com
■ David Matthews, Reliance Loan Center
www.reliancebankstl.com
■ Gary Sitton, SunGard Bi-Tech
www.bi-tech.sungardps.com
■ Randy Luebke, Nations Home Funding
www.rebiz.com/
■ Kathey Dufek, The Doctors Company
www.thedoctors.com
■ Matt Holt, John Wiley & Sons
www.wiley.com
■ Norma Strange, Ri Training
www.ritraining.com

- Gwen Gallagher, Old Republic Home Protection
  www.orhp.com
- Jim Myers, Myers Management & Capital Group
  Myersmanagement@aol.com
- Bo Calbert, McCarthy Building Companies, Inc. Southwest
  www.mccarthy.com
- Arch Granda, Grand-west and Associates
  www.grand-west.com
- Saul Blair, IPC The Hospitalist
  www.hospitalist.com
- Renee Powers, Coldwell Banker Real Estate Group
  www.reneepowers.com
- Judy Sitton, SunGard Bi-Tech
  www.bi-tech.sungardps.com
- Mike Campion, Killer Shade
  www.KillerShade.com
- Randi Smith-Todorowski, Atlas Martial Arts
  www.atlasmartialarts.com
- Mary Ellen Dalton, Health Services Advisory Group
  www.hsag.com
- Rommie Flammer, China Mist Brands
  www.chinamist.com
- Kim Silva, Fairytale Brownies
  www.Brownies.com
- Debby Raposa, MAS-Idea Source Promotions
  www.ideasourcepromotions.com
- Jeff Hurt, National Association of Dental Plans
  www.nadp.org
- Phil Singleton, John Driscoll and Company
  www.jdriscollco.com

- Susan Caldwell, *Applaud Women*
  www.applaudonline.com
- Dr. Steven Gitt, North Valley Plastic Surgery
  www.nvpsaz.com
- Betty Chan-Bauza, LifeLock
  www.lifelock.com
- Rick Labrum, SmithBarney
  www.fa.smithbarney.com/thelabrumgroupsb
- Stephanie Studds, U.S. Census Bureau
  www.census.gov
- Steve Hill, Hawgwash (U.S.Marine Corps. Master Sargeant, retired)
  www.hawgwash.biz/
- Bruce Crile, The Doctors Company
  www.thedoctors.com
- Dr. Bud Rasner, Knolls Dental Group
  www.knollsdental.com
- Ruth Covey, Armor Designs
  www.armordesigns.com
- David Rawles, Career Workshops
  www.careerworkshops.org
- Doug Ducey, iMemories
  www.imemories.com
- Marlys Foster, Mary Kay
  www.marykay.com/mfoster3516
- Rodney Covey, Department of Public Safety
  www.azdps.gov
- Dr. Geoff Haw, Sagacity Services
  www.sagacityservices.com.au/privacy

Appendix

- Michael D. Austin, Armor Sports Holdings
  www.sma-ma.net
- Stacy Tetschner, CAE—National Speakers Association
  www.nsaspeaker.org
- Dale Irvin
  www.daleirvin.com
- Penny Barrington Haw, Capacity Life Coaching
  www.capacitycoaching.com.au
- Kelly Zitlow, Surburban Mortgage
  www.kellyzitlow.com/
- John and Anne Draper, Bear Mountain Ranch, Colorado
  www.BearMountainRanch.com
- Allan T. Zinky, PMP American Express Technologies
  www.AmericanExpress.com

About the Author

Are you a Reactor Factor? Marsha Petrie Sue knows! Do you. . . React during a bad economy?

React to lousy outcomes?

React because you don't get the information you need?

React to office politics and gossip?

React because you think you're going to be laid off?

React and blame others for your lack of success?

React with an entitlement attitude?

Known as the Accountability Master, Marsha Petrie Sue, MBA, CSP, dares people to take personal responsibility for their reactions to business situations and provides information to consider and learn how to respond. As a professional speaker and author, she has been called irreverent, cheeky, sassy, smart, dynamic, clever, and a hoot. Marsha has delivered her "personal accountability" messages throughout the world via live presentation, interviews, teleseminars, articles, and webinars. She is original, unique, a one-of-a-kind professional speaker and author, and defies every morsel of your beliefs while entertaining and enlightening.

Her last book, *Toxic People: Decontaminate Difficult People at Work Without Using Weapons or Duct Tape* has been translated into Russian, Romanian, Czech, and French and is a Barnes and Noble bestseller. Her award-winning *CEO of YOU: Leading YOURSELF to Success* book also has worldwide distribution. In addition, she was awarded the CSP (Certified Speaking Professional) designation that is held by less than 600 of the speaking professionals worldwide.

Her DVDs, CDs, and audio recordings give you the tools to succeed and manage your life. Visit her web site for additional resources and for more information: www.MarshaPetrieSue.com.

You can also call, toll-free: 1.866.661.8756.

Sign up for the Personal Responsibility for Success Club on Facebook at http://t.pm0.net/s/c?6h.bkbz.1.7qpe.

You can connect with Marsha Petrie Sue in any of these ways:

BLOG: www.DecontaminateToxicPeople.com

YOUTUBE: http://t.pm0.net/s/c?6h.bl2g.7.6w4k

LINKEDIN: http://t.pm0.net/s/c?6h.bl2g.8.6w4l

PLAXO: http://t.pm0.net/s/c?6h.bl2g.9.6w4m

FACEBOOK: http://t.pm0.net/s/c?6h.bl2g.10.6yc6

TWITTER @mpsue: http://t.pm0.net/s/c?6h.bl2g.13.73cg

Marsha and her husband Al live in Scottsdale, Arizona, and get away from the summer killer heat in Arizona by retreating to their mountain cabin. They are birders, anglers, and travelers. In addition, Marsha's hobbies include photography, gardening, and golf.